# Helping Traumatized Families

The new edition of the classic *Helping Traumatized Families* not only offers clinicians a unified, evidence-based theory of the systemic impact of traumatic stress—it also details a systematic approach to helping families heal by promoting their natural healing resources. Though the impact of trauma on a family can be growth producing, some families either struggle or fail to adapt successfully. *Helping Traumatized Families* guides practitioners around common pitfalls and toward a series of evidence-based strategies that they can use to help families feel empowered and ultimately to thrive by developing tools for enhancing resilience and self-regulation.

**Charles R. Figley**, PhD, is the Paul Henry Kurzweg Distinguished Chair at Tulane University. A former Marine sergeant who served early in the Vietnam War, he went on to help pioneer the modern study of trauma and many innovations in helping the traumatized, including practitioners themselves, in his more than 200 scholarly articles, chapters, and books.

**Laurel J. Kiser**, PhD, MBA, is an associate professor at the University of Maryland School of Medicine and heads the Family Informed Trauma Treatment Center (FITT). She has been supported by NIMH and SAMHSA to develop family-based trauma interventions including Strengthening Family Coping Resources (SFCR). Her articles appear frequently in the professional literature.

ROUTLEDGE PSYCHOSOCIAL STRESS SERIES
Charles R. Figley, Ph.D., Series Editor

### Editorial Board

# Helping Traumatized Families

## Second edition

CHARLES R. FIGLEY AND LAUREL J. KISER

Routledge
Taylor & Francis Group

NEW YORK AND LONDON

First published 2013
by Routledge
711 Third Avenue, New York, NY 10017

Simultaneously published in the UK
by Routledge
27 Church Road, Hove, East Sussex BN3 2FA

*Routledge is an imprint of the Taylor & Francis Group, an informa business*

© 2013 Charles R. Figley and Laurel J. Kiser

The right of Charles R. Figley and Laurel J. Kiser to be identified as
authors of this work has been asserted by them in accordance with
sections 77 and 78 of the Copyright, Designs and Patents Act 1988.

This book is part of the Psychosocial Stress Series, edited by Charles Figley.

*Library of Congress Cataloging in Publication Data*
Figley, Charles R., 1944–
   Helping traumatized families / Charles R. Figley and Laurel J. Kiser. —
   2nd ed.
      p. cm. — (Routledge psychosocial stress series)
    Includes bibliographical references and index.
   1. Post-traumatic stress disorder.  2. Families—Mental health.
   3. Family psychotherapy.  I. Kiser, Laurel J., 1955–  II. Title.
   RC552.P67F54 2013
   618.92′8521—dc23                           2012019297

ISBN: 978–0–415–89445–6 (hbk)
ISBN: 978–0–415–63884–5 (pbk)
ISBN: 978–0–203–81350–8 (ebk)

Typeset in Minion
by Swales & Willis Ltd, Exeter, Devon

Printed and bound in the United States of America
by Edwards Brothers, Inc.

# Contents

# Series Editor's Foreword

The Routledge Psychosocial Stress Series welcomes this latest edition. *Helping Traumatized Families* was originally published by Jossey-Bass, a San Francisco-based publisher. Over the years it became one of the most frequently cited in both scholarly and practice literature about families. It was among the few that focused both on trauma and on families.

This series started with the 1978 publication of *Stress Disorders Among Vietnam Veterans* with Brunner/Mazel. As a publisher, Brunner/Mazel helped found the modern study of traumatology. Their editors were particularly focused on the immediate and long-term psychosocial and behavioral indicators and consequences of trauma and the most efficacious approaches to minimizing the damage and promoting resilience and growth.

The second edition of *Helping Traumatized Families* is not the first book in the series to focus on understanding and helping families. The second and third books of the series, *Stress and the Family*, volume 1 (focusing on developmental markers) and volume 2 (focusing on trauma and catastrophe), were the first to bring research and treatment together in one volume as well as an understanding of traumatic stress and developmental crisis and combining our emerging knowledge about both trauma and family, as does this book. *Treating Stress in Families* was published the same year as *Helping Traumatized Families*, and both were especially interested in trauma, stress, and how both manifest themselves within the family system.

In that same year, 1989, the series welcomed *Systemic Treatment of Incest: A Therapeutic Handbook*, coauthored by Terry Trepper and Mary Jo Barrett. It was the first book actually to focus the entire text on incest and its treatment. The specialty was in its infancy.

Three years later the series welcomed *Coping With Infant or Fetal Loss: The Couple's Healing Process*, by Kathleen Gilbert and Laura Smart. It was the first to describe the adaptation of couples using a systemic family functioning paradigm.

In 2004 Don Catherall wrote the first of two books for the series. The first, *Handbook of Stress, Trauma, and the Family*, was a first-of-its-kind compendium of theories, research findings, and treatment methods specifically for traumatized families. Catherall was one of the first to focus on the busy practitioner who needed clear guidelines and strategies for helping these families. The next year he edited the follow-up book for the series, *Family Stressors: Interventions for Stress and Trauma*. This book focused on the additional treatment approaches that emerged to help detect and manage family stressors.

Finally, in 2010, the series welcomed *Families Under Fire: Systemic Therapy With Military Families*, which I coedited with Blaine Everson. It not only combined family and trauma but also addressed the many issues confronting service members and their families.

This revised edition of *Helping Traumatized Families*, therefore, continues a long line of extraordinary books that help us understand traumatized families enough to facilitate resilience.

Charles R. Figley, Ph.D., Series Editor
Tulane University, New Orleans, USA

# Preface to the 1989 Edition

*Editorial Note: This preface was written in approximately 1987. The term "PTSD" had been coined in 1980. In 1978, the first book of the Psychosocial Stress Series discussed the psychosocial consequences of trauma, and practitioners were looking for practical advice based on the emerging scientific and professional understanding of trauma and its systemic consequences. This preface provides a useful window into that era and how and why* Helping Traumatized Families *was published in the first place.*

How would you feel if you and your family were suddenly struggling with a situation you had never thought was possible? For example, how would you cope if your child were diagnosed with an incurable disease that left you and your family devastated, angry, confused, and hopeless? Perhaps you and your family have already experienced times of chaos and disillusionment, though they may not have lasted very long. Those of us who have experienced such times struggle along as best we can, not sure that we are coping as well as we might.

For nearly two decades I have worked with traumatized families dealing with a variety of stressful situations. My successes have outnumbered my failures, but there clearly were failures, particularly in the beginning.

I began to write this book in 1972, soon after my first professional work with a traumatized family. I am not sure why it has taken so long to complete it. Perhaps it is because I did not have enough to say until now or perhaps because I failed miserably with that first client family and have never quite recovered from it—I was traumatized, as it were.

Completing this book ends what has been for me quite a long and, at times, lonely journey. It began with a personal concern for the welfare of the families of American veterans of the Vietnam War, shifted to a concentration on the families of Americans held hostage in Iran, and expanded to include an examination of families exposed to a variety of catastrophes: natural and man-made disasters, criminal assaults, inter- and intrafamily abuse, death, and terminal illness.

Now that I have completed the book I can turn my attention more fully to other issues and topics that also capture my attention. But none will ever be more important to me than my interest in families struggling to overcome memories of horror. I hope I have made at least a small contribution toward the alleviation of their suffering.

## Overview of the Contents

In writing *Helping Traumatized Families* I hoped to fulfill at least three objectives: (1) to review what we know about traumatized families, including definitions of some important concepts and several theoretical models that clarify them; (2) to discuss the ways families typically cope with trauma, including both functional and dysfunctional patterns of coping; and (3) to describe a comprehensive approach to treating traumatized families. The book's content is consistent with these objectives.

In Chapter one I focus on how and why I view families as systems of interacting relationships. I expand on this perspective in the next several chapters by describing the building blocks of my theory of traumatized family processes. Also in the first chapter I define what I mean by trauma and who I believe constitute "traumatized families." I continue in Chapter one to emphasize the universality of trauma—many more people, and thus families, are traumatized than we once thought.

In Chapter two I address the second objective of the book. I note how important families are to all of us and show how families have natural and remarkably effective ways of helping traumatized members (detecting traumatic stress, urging confrontation of the stressor, urging recapitulation of the catastrophe, and facilitating resolution of the conflicts). I also review the ways in which families are naturally supportive of their members. Indeed, families are so effective and efficient in helping traumatized members that I have tailored my approach to treating families on the basis of these naturally existing methods. These methods include clarifying insights, correcting distortions, and supporting alternative perspectives.

In Chapter two I introduce a way of summarizing the powerful role families play in human functioning and the process by which the family system confronts and recovers from trauma. This family adaptation model incorporates research from many studies of families exposed to highly stressful experiences. Chapter two provides a context that conveys an appreciation of the variety of ways in which families cope with stressors and clarifies the characteristics that differentiate functional from dysfunctional family coping.

The remaining chapters address the third objective of the book.

In Chapter three I present the theoretical building blocks for my approach to conceptualizing, assessing, and treating traumatized families. In my work I attempt to empower the family members to make peace with the past and take charge of their lives. This kind of intervention could be categorized as primary as well as secondary prevention. In addition to helping families make peace with the past, I educate them about trauma, traumatic stress, family functioning, and recovery. Moreover, I attempt to enhance their natural resources, including their basic family social skills and supportiveness.

In Chapter four I present my approach to evaluating the family system client, beginning with a detailed description of the clinical interview, and then describe several useful standardized measures of stress, traumatic stress, social support, and family pathology.

The remainder of the book focuses on the empowerment approach to helping traumatized families. In Chapter five I describe and justify the eight basic clinical objectives for helping traumatized families and include a detailed description of my five-phase approach to empowering traumatized families.

In Chapters six through ten I describe each of these phases in detail: Phase One (Chapter six) is building commitment to the therapeutic objectives, Phase Two (Chapter seven) is framing the problem, Phase Three (Chapter eight) is reframing the problem, Phase Four (Chapter nine) is developing a healing theory, and Phase Five (Chapter ten) is closure and preparedness.

Chapter eleven is devoted entirely to a discussion of helping traumatized children, beginning with a section focusing on developmental issues and including a list of children's methods for coping with trauma. Most of the chapter, however, focuses on methods useful in helping children within a family context.

In the final chapter, Chapter twelve, I return to my objectives for the book in an effort to summarize the major points. I also discuss the special nature of traumatized families, the emerging field that specializes in their study and care, and the special challenges to research, treatment, and the practitioner in working with this special population.

Included as resources at the end of the book are three questionnaires. The Traumagram Questionnaire (Resource A) and the Purdue Post-Traumatic Stress Disorder Scale (Resource B) are useful in identifying the existence and severity of traumatic events. The Purdue Social Support Scale (Resource C) can help the practitioner to assess the quality and quantity of social support among client family members.

## Audience

I wrote *Helping Traumatized Families* with practitioners in mind—those who struggle on a regular basis to help families, particularly traumatized families: psychologists, psychiatrists and other physicians, nurses, clergy, social workers, and family therapists. If the book fulfills my intended goals, it will become a primary resource for identifying and assisting individuals and families coping with trauma. A secondary audience may be students being trained to work with traumatized families or individuals.

Thus it is my hope that this book will become the primary reference for the assessment and treatment of those traumatized by a wide variety of stressors. I hope it will help practitioners identify, empathize with, and generally understand traumatized individuals and families and the interactions among family members.

Academic readers (especially students) will be more interested in the first half of the book, which focuses on the scientific literature and description of the problem. Indeed, this book draws on the separate literatures of cognitive and behavioral psychology, crisis intervention, traumatic stress, family therapy, disaster/traumatic stress, and community mental health in general. However, this book fits well within the growing area of specialization on family stress and coping.

Mostly, I hope that this book will provide a sense of inspiration and motivation for working with frightened and confused people, those traumatized by one or more circumstances. The book emerged from my experiences with hundreds of traumatized people and families. Out of their lives and their courage emerged a perspective that has helped me help them. At the same time, they have given me an appreciation of their special struggles and extraordinary achievements.

# Preface

We have come a long way in the fifteen years since this book was published. When it was time to revise it my publisher, Anna Moore at Routledge, and I agreed that Laurel Kiser was the perfect co-author and someone who could bring her many talents to help this updated version reflect the extraordinary progress made by both researchers and practitioners since the late 1980s.

Here I will try to provide some information to serve as a bridge from the first edition of *Helping Traumatized Families* (HTF1) and the current edition of the book (HTF2). The first volume attempted to provide a general orientation to helping traumatized individuals by educating her or his family about the phases of adaptation, the common symptoms, and the strategies for helping them at each phase.

Also, HTF2 offers a model that includes but goes beyond the one presented in HTF1. The Family Adaptation to Trauma Model provides a roadmap to the reader about the critical elements within the traumatized family that indicates the degree to which the family is functioning. The model includes what we think is an innovative way of representing how well families are functioning: An Adaptation Meter indicates where a family falls from low (failing) to high (thriving). It is a kind of spectrum-oriented yardstick that provides a general indicator of how the family is functioning compared to other families in similar circumstances.

HTF2 includes most of the materials covered in HTF1 but with more updated references and conclusions that help practitioners more effectively assess and treat families. This guidance includes the Family Adaptation Model and its Adaptation Meter.

The book is divided into three parts. Part one, "Understanding the Impact of Trauma on Families," includes three chapters. The first chapter, "The Family as a Living System," discusses the overall functioning of families generally, over history, time, culture, and circumstances. The next chapter (Chapter two) is about individual responses to trauma and how individuals behave within families and their own skin, and how the traumatic stress symptoms, such as lack of sound sleep, affect and infect the sanctity, civility, and security of family life. This leads to the final chapter in Part one, "Spreading Beyond the Individual: Family Adaptation to Stress and Trauma" (Chapter three), which discusses the fundamental impact of trauma and traumatic memories on the family through its members' traumatic experiences and memories.

Part two, "Empowering Families," includes five phases, discussed in turn in Chapters five to nine. Collectively they describe many strategies for facilitating recovery and resilience in families and their members. Chapter four, "Foundations of the Empowerment Treatment Approach," discusses the theory, research, and components of the empowerment approach. Chapter five describes Phase I, Joining the Family, as establishing a knowing and trusting relationship with the family. Chapter six covers Phase II, Understanding and Framing the Family's Trauma Response, which requires the family therapist to be effective in assessing the family and developing the treatment goals collaboratively, and families to be committed to the treatment plan. Chapter seven covers Phase III, Building Healing Skills, which guides the therapist to build the critical skills that lead to healing: listening, speaking from the heart, and demonstrating support and love, among many. Chapter eight continues this effort through Phase IV, Sharing and Healing. Family members learn to share and other family members not only learn to listen accurately but learn to listen in ways that emphasize their love and support. The final phase of the empowering approach, Phase V, Moving Forward, covered in Chapter nine, is about being reminded how far the family has come—emotionally and as a family team—since they first sought help. This chapter outlines what it is important to cover before saying good-bye, which includes anticipating future traumatic experiences and best practices for facilitating family resilience.

The final part of the book is called "Empowering Family Trauma Therapists," which is what we attempt to do in these final chapters. Chapter ten, "The Family Trauma Therapist," emphasizes the highly stressful nature of working with the traumatized and especially traumatized families. The final chapter, Chapter eleven, "Epilogue: Implications for Practice, Policy, and Research," is an effort to consider the book, the previous edition, and the current and future of efforts to understand and help families cope with trauma.

Laurel and I do hope that this book will continue to serve as a critical resource for those of you who read it, and that this book will serve as a source of reassurance to practitioners and families alike of the double challenge of working with both trauma and families. We hope that both practitioners and clients recognize that there is considerable leeway for creativity and the occasional failure.

Charles R. Figley

# Acknowledgments

The authors would like to acknowledge Anna Moore of Routledge, who assisted us with all aspects of this new edition of *Helping Traumatized Families*. Our reviewers were very helpful in recognizing the gems contained in the original version and what could be added that would be most useful in helping the traumatized. We appreciate the assistance of Vicky Lattone and Alicia McCaw toward the end of the project. Finally, we especially want to acknowledge our supportive spouses, Kathy Regan Figley and David Pruitt, who were our primary support system throughout this project.

# Part one

# Understanding the Impact of Trauma on Families

# one
# The Family as a Living System

## Family as a Dynamic System

Throughout nature, plants, insects, animals, and humans join together to form systems. Take for example a stand of trees (as excerpted from "The way we stand" by Susan Griffin, 1991):

> The way we stand, you can see we have grown up this way together, out of the same soil, with the same rains, leaning in the same way towards the sun. See how we lean together in the same direction. How the dead limbs of one of us rest in the branches of another. How those branches have grown around the limbs. How the two are inseparable . . . and in the way we stand, each alone, yet none of us separable, none of us beautiful when separate but all exquisite as we stand, each moment heeded in this cycle, no detail unlovely.

For human beings, families are the most obvious of social systems. Social systems are webs of relationships that form predictable patterns of interactions with numerous, measurable byproducts that represent the will of the system or a significant subsystem.

All systems are dynamic. In a stand of trees, when one tree falls, all of the other trees are changed. Family is a similar kind of dynamic system connected not by roots and branches but by interpersonal relationships that account for changes in behaviors of family members. Families and trees must adapt to changes—be they sudden and dangerous or gradual but profound. This is one way to illustrate how families are living systems (Kiser, 2008). We view families as strong and resilient systems able to change and adapt to most of life's circumstances. We also know that some life circumstances can overwhelm a family system. When trauma occurs, some families will have trouble adapting in healthy and sustainable ways.

As stated in the Preface to the 1989 Edition, we have three main objectives for this book: (1) to review what we know about families who have experienced trauma, including definitions of some important concepts and several theoretical models that clarify them; (2) to discuss the typical ways families cope with trauma, by presenting a model of family adaptation to trauma; and (3) to describe a comprehensive approach to treating a variety of families suffering from the aftershocks of their trauma.

We have worked with families impacted by trauma over several decades and have felt their pain, marveled at their resilience, and celebrated with them as they recovered. We hope that this book will provide a way to view and help *both* the person and the family (or other social system) as they cope with their trauma experiences.

## The Systemic Nature of Family Trauma

We would like to introduce you to the Murrays. They will be your guide through this book as we review their case and their progress through family trauma treatment.

## The Murray Family

Mary Murray (all names here are fictitious) was jolted from her thoughts by a coworker's announcement: "Mary, Tammy's principal needs to speak with you right away." Mr. Perez informed Mary that her eleven-year-old daughter had been overheard saying she was planning to commit suicide.

After consultation with the school counselor, Tammy was referred to a local psychotherapist for evaluation. After one session with the therapist, it was recommended that the rest of the family join her: her parents, John and Mary, and her nine-year-old brother, Tim. The clinician determined that Tammy was under considerable stress from the pressures of school and home. At the same time the clinician hypothesized that the family was in a state of shock, traumatized by a series of stressful jolts that had been building for months and were now culminating in Tammy's suicide talk.

John, the father, had recently sought treatment for "exhaustion," although by all previous indications he had been the model of a happy and productive executive. But in the last six weeks his life had been in shambles. He had been able to sleep only a few hours each night. He had missed more work this past month (because of various minor illnesses) than at any time in his life. He felt jumpy and irritable and fluctuated between feeling apathetic and enraged. According to Mary, his wife of fifteen years, he was no longer interested in the things that once brought him joy: his children, Little League coaching, fishing, and photography.

What was most troublesome to John, however, was his re-experiencing of several troubling memories of past events. These events had occurred over fifteen years ago when he was a corpsman in the war in Vietnam. Although he had not thought much about the war since returning home, he was now experiencing both daydreams and nightmares of the war almost daily. He had tried to talk about these experiences with Mary. She listened and tried to encourage John to put his memories behind him for the good of his family and himself. He tried to forget the past but could not. Moreover, he was unable to recall certain periods of time during his yearlong tour of duty in the war. He was frightened, confused, and concerned that his boss and coworkers would think he was unable to function effectively in his extremely responsible position.

In the last few years Mary had threatened divorce, was frequently depressed, had difficulty sleeping, and was probably abusing alcohol. Both Tim and Tammy had been extremely upset and were more and more depressed about what had been happening to their family. They both were doing poorly in school, tending to avoid being at home with their father, and fighting among themselves more frequently. Both felt that, if they were better children, they could help their family and parents out of this situation.

The family had struggled along this way for weeks, until Tammy's depression led to her thoughts about suicide. The family assembled for treatment, at first to focus their attention on Tammy's depression. Soon, however, they would be dealing with other stressors that had culminated in a family system impacted by trauma.

Fortunately, the clinician was able to see beyond Tammy's suicide talk to recognize that it might be symptomatic of a traumatized family.

Most often families who have been traumatized go unnoticed. They are viewed as the "victim's family." Families who have experienced trauma often feel alone and reluctant to seek help outside the family. In the last decade human service systems have recognized that, unless we attend to the social network of the victim, the victim will not recover quickly from her or his stressful experiences. Yet, as a result of the traumatic experiences, the network (most often the "victim" is the family) can barely handle routine matters and may be unable to help members struggling to recover emotionally.

The Murray family illustrates how systems, particularly family systems, work. Even though much of the trauma can be traced to the father's experiences and in particular to the family's reactions to his efforts to handle his memories, it is none the less traumatic for each family member. As with so many families, the struggles of each member of the Murray family are easy to see but are much more complex and effectively helped when viewed in a broader family context.

## Viewing Families Impacted by Trauma

Families who have been traumatized are those who are attempting to cope with an extraordinary stressor or stressors that have disrupted their normal life routine in unwanted ways. The connectedness of family members with one another is why they are so vulnerable to stress, particularly traumatic stress. When one person in a family—or any semi-closed system, such as a fraternity or sorority, a card club, or a submarine crew—is upset, this upset is sensed by others in the system. Almost immediately efforts are made to correct the problem: eliminate the stressor, ease the distress, or find an effective coping method. So it is with families coping with trauma.

A family impacted by trauma, then, is struggling to recover from and to cope with an injury or wound to its system. As will be noted later, this "injury" can happen in many different ways and at various levels of intensity. The "injury" could range from a seemingly small incident that would be a minor annoyance to another family to the death or extraordinary abuse of one or more family members. What is most critical, however, is the fact that the trauma experienced by one family member may be experienced by the entire family system. Thus, families who have been traumatized are injured systemically and are vulnerable to a wide variety of systemic dysfunction.

Family trauma is also complicated by the fact that it is not uncommon for the family or another family member to be *responsible* for the trauma, as in the case of incest. In this case, the "injury" is caused by the family. Trauma is both a cause and a consequence, and the family can either be a source of support and healing (see Chapter two) or cause additional harm (for example, when they refuse to believe the abuse happened or blame the victim for what happened). The bulk of the material in this book focuses on the system of the family who has been traumatized and on how best to detect and help these families.

Most importantly, trauma represents in families their shared memories of experiencing one or a series of sudden and overwhelming adversities requiring adaptation and management. Critical to the family's reaction are the beliefs, points of view, perceptions, frames of reference, or cognitive appraisals of family members—both separately and collectively.

Helping families who have been traumatized, then, is empowering the family collectively to process or take into their awareness what they have experienced. By doing so they eventually figure out a way to work out conflicts, fears, and intentions within the family; the family can exchange perspectives that enable them sufficiently to understand, accept, and adapt to others' reactions collectively (as a system, as a family).

## Conclusion

There has been extraordinary growth in the field of traumatology, the study and treatment of trauma, especially in the areas of individual assessments (Wilson & Keane, 2004), evidence-based treatments (Ursano et al., 2004), and the evidence-based models that guide them (Figley, 2002a). Growth in understanding families impacted by trauma has been modest and slow to translate into practice.

What accounts for this slow growth and development in helping families dealing with trauma is that most funding sources and treating practitioners are trained to work with individuals. Hospitals, clinics, schools, and all things government are oriented to people not systems. But the most important reason why development has been slow is the complicated nature of studying families generally. Families are far more difficult to understand, predict, and help. They are far more than a collection of individuals. Families, no less families who have been traumatized, are fascinating, and every one is unique (Figley, 1978, 1998).

Many term-laden systemic concepts have emerged over the years, particularly in family therapy theory, to identify the various components and functions within the family system. We have consciously tried to avoid such terms and other professional jargon. In addition to wanting the most coherent book possible on helping families who have been traumatized, we also wish to write one that appeals to colleagues from various disciplines, theoretical orientations, cultures, and languages. We hope that this chapter is an indication that what we are trying to do with this second edition is to make it as accessible as possible to all.

# two
# Individual Responses to Trauma

When families experience high stress and trauma, the whole family system reacts. Individual family members are affected, as are all the other parts of the family. Yet the primary focus of researchers and practitioners in traumatology is on individual trauma experiences and reactions. To appreciate the importance of families in the context of individual experiences of trauma and recovery, it is critical first to understand how individuals respond to trauma.

Interestingly, the study of traumatic stress began with the earliest medical writings in 1900 B.C. in the first discussion of what would later be described as hysteria (Veith, 1965). Trimble (1981) has provided an important history of traumatic stress that demonstrates the intense interest in this area, particularly within Western culture from the sixteenth century to the present.

The area of stress and coping seemed to evolve separately from that of traumatic stress, however, with Claude Bernard's (Selye, 1956) focus on the *milieu intérieur*, or internal environment, of a living organism, the importance of which remains fairly constant irrespective of its external environment. Walter B. Cannon (1939) built on the concept of "homeostasis," the ability of the body to remain in a constant state, providing staying power.

Hans Selye (1956), in one of the earliest conceptualizations of stress, defined stress as the "state manifested by a specific syndrome which consists of all the nonspecifically-induced changes within a biologic system" (p. 64). Later he defined stress more simply: "The nonspecific response of the body to any demand made upon it" (Selye, 1974, p. 14). Even more helpful than his attempts to define stress was Selye's discovery of the biological stress syndrome, or general adaptation syndrome (GAS), which describes the body's general method of coping with any type of stressor. Briefly, the syndrome includes three phases. The alarm reaction involves the body's initially reacting to a stressor. Most often the body adjusts and, through the resistance phase, draws on its energy reserves to cope with the stressor. All indicators of stress exhibited in the alarm phase have disappeared. However, with repeated exposure to a stressor, the body enters the final phase, exhaustion. Here the body exhausts its adaptive energy; the signs of the alarm phase reappear, but now they are irreversible, and unless something is done quickly death may occur.

Trauma is defined as "an injury (as a wound) to living tissue caused by an extrinsic agent; disordered psychic or behavioral state resulting from mental or emotional stress or physical injury." The analogy of a physical wound is not always directly applicable to either people or systems such as families, yet it is a useful metaphor for appreciating the process by which we respond to particular stressors over many years. More recently, for example, Figley and Nash (2007) have argued that prior to a combat-related mental disorder such as clinical depression, posttraumatic stress disorder (PTSD), and others there is a clear and discernible psychological stress injury. The emergence of an injury is a limited window of opportunity to promote resilience and prevent these illnesses from developing. Results of recent studies suggest that it is common for patients to have some posttraumatic symptoms one year after a burn injury and that early experiences of posttraumatic stress symptoms may be associated with the development or maintenance of posttraumatic stress disorder (Ehde, Patterson, Wiechman, & Wilson, 2000).

Currently, trauma is understood in terms of a complex biopsychosocial response system. At the biological level, this response involves the central nervous system (CNS) and the endocrine and immune systems. "In response to stress, the hypothalamus releases corticotrophin releasing hormone (CRF), which influences the pituitary gland to secrete adrenocorticotropic hormone, which, in turn, stimulates the adrenal cortex to release corticosteroids" (Repetti, Taylor, & Seeman, 2002, p. 337). Threat creates a shifting balance between autonomic systems that prepare the organism for action (the sympathetic nervous system) and for retreat or rest once the threat is removed (the parasympathetic nervous system). We know, now, that cycling through this stress response system when faced with mild stressors is important for physical health and well-being, but that exposure to trauma or chronic high stress (and the associated stress hormones) is related to physical and mental health problems (Southwick, Morgan, Vythilingam, Krystal, & Charney, 2004). At the psychological level, the response to stress and trauma involves attention to and appraisal of the threat and activation of both short- and long-term coping efforts. Importantly, for those working with families, the biological and psychological responses to stress and trauma are dependent on social context. As human beings, our complex reactions to threat are heavily influenced by the presence of others and especially others with whom we share a close bond.

## Coping with Stress and Trauma

As human beings, we all learn to cope with stressors of varying types with varying degrees of effectiveness. As early as the first month of life, infants begin to develop methods of coping with stress. New and more complex patterns of behavior evolve. An infant who looks long and hard at a new object before reaching for it is also the toddler who stands in the nursery school doorway and watches the other children before joining their play (Murphy & Moriarty, 1976).

Across the life span, we learn and use coping skills to adjust to stressors and traumas. Compas, Connor-Smith, Saltzman, Thomsen, and Wadsworth (2001) define coping as "successful adaptation to stress," which includes "the ways in which individuals manage their emotions, think constructively, regulate and direct their behavior, control their autonomic arousal, and act on the social and nonsocial environments to alter or decrease sources of stress" (p. 127).

Individuals use a variety of methods for coping with stress—be it traumatic or nontraumatic. These might include emotional strategies (e.g., crying, humor, anger), cognitive strategies (e.g., denial, distraction, needing to know what happened, anticipation), problem-focused strategies (e.g., reducing the stressful conditions), and social strategies (e.g., solace seeking, altruism) (Berg, Meegan, & Deviney, 1998; Winje, 1998). Congruence models suggest that coping is most effective when a variety of coping schemas or styles are within the individual's or family's skill set and appraisal of threat and stressor dimensions leads to activation of a corresponding coping schema (Peacock & Wong, 1996).

## Coping Strategies

We discuss a variety of coping strategies frequently used by individuals who have experienced trauma. Taking into account a developmental life span approach, special considerations for coping by children are included below in italics. Children also use some additional coping strategies (fantasy/play, acting out, and regression) that are consistent with their cognitive and emotional development. It is important for family-centered clinicians to know that (1) the early development of coping takes place primarily within the context of interactions among an infant and her or his parents and (2) the coping styles used by parents and the family are determinants of children's responses and significantly influence coping. In other words, children learn to cope by watching and interacting with their parents.

## Emotional Coping

**Crying.** Crying is frequently chosen as a method for coping with highly stressful experiences. For many individuals it brings relief to overwhelming emotions. It is also a way of bringing attention to anxiety and pain and needed comfort and reassurance. *For children: Although crying is extremely upsetting to parents, children frequently cry more following exposure to trauma. Crying is an especially effective communication for drawing parents and caregivers closer and encouraging affection.*

**Anger.** Anger is an emotion frequently associated with stressful conditions and trauma. Especially in cases in which individuals must cope with an ongoing traumatic experience involving interpersonal violence, anger and rage may result. Early on this response was thought to be related to "identification with the aggressor" or the "Stockholm syndrome" (Eitinger, 1982). It was named after the young female bank clerks held hostage in a Stockholm bank robbery who, after being released, attacked the police and defended the criminals. *For children: When children must cope with an ongoing traumatic experience, such as child abuse—inside or outside the home by an adult or a child—they may defend the abuser and also begin to act like her or him. Aggressive play or increased fighting may be ways that children express their anger.*

**Humor.** Individuals use humor to cope with stress: expressing pain, fear, disappointment, frustration, anger, neediness. Often humor is a means of distraction rather than a way of seeking some resolution of the crisis or stressful situation. It also is associated with positive emotions and may bring relief from the constant experience of fear, worry, or sadness associated with traumatic distress. *For children: Humor takes different forms, of course, depending on the age of the child. Younger children utilize more physical methods, in contrast to older children, who are more intellectual and complicated in their use of humor.*

## Cognitive Coping

**Denial.** Denial is one of the most frequently used methods of coping with stress for both adults and children. By refusing to believe that the stressful situation exists or that they or their loved ones are affected, they are able to avoid the costs of such a situation. Used in moderation, this form of coping can be quite adaptive. Denial provides a needed cognitive respite from worry about overwhelmingly stressful circumstances. *For children: Wishful thinking may be a form of denial used by children. Using this strategy, they can choose to believe that the trauma did not happen, that the losses they suffered are not real or permanent, or that a happy ending is still possible.*

**Distraction.** Here individuals choose to focus on other things. By thinking of other things, they find relief from unpleasant, "scary and lucky" thoughts associated with the traumatic events. As Scarlett O'Hara said in *Gone With the Wind*, "I'll think about that tomorrow." Adults may distract themselves by becoming engrossed in their work or hobbies. *For children: Children may* *become engrossed in typical activities, such as computer games or videotapes. For other children, it may be fantasy games with dolls or cars.*

**Need to Know What Happened.** Many individuals focus on the facts. They want to know every detail of what happened. This usually means that they talk a lot about the trauma and rehash every aspect of the event. *For children: Children may also become engrossed in the details of what happened. This may be translated into posttraumatic play where the event is rehearsed over and over again.*

**Anticipation.** By foreseeing and planning for other stressful events, individuals feel more prepared and, thus, more in control of their lives. *For children: "What if you die, Mummy?" is a common question from children who experience the death of someone in their life. Often parents discourage anticipation and such questions out of concern that the preparation may be worse than what actually happens. But preparation rarely is worse. Children seek structure, control, and security in their lives, particularly during or following a highly stressful event.*

## Problem-Focused Coping

**Reducing the Stressful Conditions.** Many times individuals actively engage in tasks related to resolving the circumstances that are causing stress. A good example of this would be the individual who has lost his or her home following a hurricane and focuses much of his or her attention and energy on making the necessary arrangements to move his or her family into new housing. *For children: Children may also utilize problem-focused coping strategies that are consistent with their age and stage of development.*

## Social Coping

**Seeking Solace.** Some individuals cope with stress by reaching out to others. They look for extra attention, kindness, and special favors. *For children: Children can seek solace in some interesting ways. One is by becoming clingy and having trouble separating from their parents or caregivers. Another is to feign illness. Most children associate being sick with special care. Parents or caregivers stay close and bring them special food and sometimes new toys or books to help them pass the time. These special favors received by sick children are things that might be helpful for some children in coping with highly stressful experiences. They may be unable or unwilling to ask for these things as a way of coping with stress, but think that they can get them by pretending to be sick.*

**Altruism.** Struggling with their own distress, some individuals look for ways to give to others. They may suddenly become extremely helpful and useful to other family members and friends or become involved in volunteerism. This too enables them to forget about their troubles and utilize signs of appreciation as a way of recovering from stressful circumstances. *For children: Children can find special ways of giving to others, especially to other family members who are distressed. A child offering a doll to another child in distress is an example.*

**Withdrawal.** Some individuals do not seek support and, in fact, prefer to deal with stress and trauma alone. They may spend less time with family and friends, sometimes to the point of becoming isolated. *For children: Children may withdraw from normally "fun" activities or lose interest in their favorite toys or playthings. Even when children are not physically withdrawn from family activities, they may succeed in withdrawing psychologically, appearing preoccupied or in a daze.*

### Additional Childhood Coping Strategies

**Fantasy/Play.** Some children cope by pretending they are somewhere else, are with someone else, or *are* someone else. Some children, for example, adopt fantasy friends or treat toys as real people in place of family members and friends. Many children use fantasy play to re-enact their traumatic experience. They often repeat these play themes over and over.

**Regression.** Children also may act as though they are younger than they are, becoming more dependent, demanding, childish, and uncooperative. A six-year-old may start sucking her thumb or wetting the bed. A three-year-old may demand to use a high chair or diapers again. Similar to the situation with illness, they may be seeking additional comfort, reassurance, and predictability in their life that only a loving parent can provide.

**Acting Out.** Another way of gaining attention and thereby avoiding the reality and consequences of the stressful experiences is impulsively acting out. This involves sudden and purposive violations of family or household rules, school or community codes, rules, or laws. Often this acting out is an imme- diate way of shifting attention to the violation and away from efforts to cope with the stressors.

An especially good example of how children cope with "stressful" experiences happened in our household some years ago, when my (CRF) younger daughter, Laura, first experienced, at three years of age, the absence of her older sister, Jessica, who was visiting her grandparents in Florida. Jessica had called home in tears because of a conflict with her grandmother. Laura first wanted to know all about Florida and why Jessica was so upset (Need To Know What Happened). Then she chose to watch several of her favorite videotapes (Distraction). She cried for a while, exclaiming how she missed her sister, when we refused to give her another piece of candy before dinner (Crying). Later we overheard her explaining to her "baby," Elizabeth the duck, why Jessica was gone and that she would be back soon (Fantasy). Laura utilized a variety of coping methods to deal with a stressful event. I doubt if Laura realized that she had chosen these activities to help her deal with her anxiety over Jessica's being gone.

# Stress Disorders

Most people experience trauma during their lifetime (Breslau, Chilcoat, Kessler, & Davis, 1999; Kessler, Sonnega, Bromet, Hughes, & Nelson, 1995; Resnick, Kilpatrick, Dansky, Saunders, & Best, 1993) and potentially detrimental effects to mental and physical health, as well as to economic welfare (S. D. Solomon & Davidson, 1997). For some individuals who have experienced trauma their coping strategies are adaptive and they are able to return to normal functioning after a short period of readjustment. For others, owing to a variety of risk and protective factors, they have a more difficult time adjusting and may develop stress-related disorders. When compared with exposure rates, a much smaller percentage develops a stress disorder such as PTSD, with a lifetime prevalence rate of approximately 8% in the United States (Kessler et al., 1995). An important gender difference exists. Resnick et al. (1993) in their survey of 4,089 U.S. adult women found that, based on the previous six-month period, lifetime exposure to any type of traumatic event was 69%, whereas exposure to crimes that included sexual or aggravated assault or homicide of a close relative or friend occurred among 36%. Overall sample prevalence of PTSD was 12.3% lifetime and 4.6% prevalence (within the past six months) rate.

So why do some individuals develop traumatic stress disorders and others do not? The traumatic event, itself, has a lot to do with it. Factors like whether someone actually died, who or what caused the event or events to occur, and how close the individual was to the violence or destruction make a big difference. Table 2.1 outlines the risks and protective factors that have been found in research to explain why not everyone exposed to a trauma suffers with PTSD. Again from a developmental life span perspective, we know that risk and protective factors differ according to the age. We discuss some of the special circumstances related to risk and protective factors in families and children next.

**TABLE 2.1.**  Risks and Protective Factors for PTSD

| Risks | Protective Factors |
|---|---|
| Female gender | Higher intellectual ability |
| Younger age at first exposure* | Biological and genetic resilience |
| General childhood adversity* | Greater access to informal resources |
| Past history of trauma | Flexible coping skills |
| Degree of exposure/loss* | Family and social support |
| Pre-existing psychiatric disorder | Family income and its purchase of |
| Parental psychopathology* | formal (professional) resources |
| Parents' degree of distress* | Knowledge of family member over |
| Family chaos, violence* | time and in adversity that can |
| Peritraumatic psychological processes | mitigate problems |

* Special consideration for children and adolescents.

As can be seen from the list of risks and protective factors in Table 2.1, families provide a protective function for individuals but can also add to the risk that their exposed members will develop PTSD. In many ways and as is commonly seen, the risk factors related to family and PTSD suggest the cyclical nature of early exposure to childhood adversity, maltreatment, and family violence. Once exposed at a young age to this type of trauma, individuals are vulnerable to significant mental health and substance abuse concerns, relational difficulties, and high risk of re-exposure to interpersonal violence, which in turn leads to a perpetuation of family chaos and violence in the next generation.

Another risk factor with implications for family functioning is the higher risk of PTSD in females. This is significant, as females often take the lead in managing daily family life and in caring for the children.

There are also specific risk factors associated with the development of PTSD in children. These include: (1) exposure to trauma and other adverse circumstances at a young age; (2) the child experiences the loss of a significant attachment figure; (3) parents' reactions are extremely disturbed; (4) the caretaker's parenting abilities are disrupted for some reason; (5) the family atmosphere is chaotic, non-supportive, or violent.

When children are exposed to trauma early in life, they face increased risk for re-exposure, development of PTSD, and ongoing functional impairments, including substance abuse, delinquency, suicidality, acts of self-destruction, chronic anger, unstable relationships, and physical health problems. The Adverse Childhood Events study clearly demonstrates the exponential increase in risk associated with multiple exposures during childhood (Felitti & Anda, 2009).

The death of a family member, especially a parent, places all children at high risk for PTSD and other emotional disturbances. Osterweis and Townsend (1988) have observed that the following factors increase the risk of long-term negative outcomes following the death of a parent or sibling:

- loss when the child is under five years of age or in early adolescence;
- loss of mother for girls under eleven and loss of father for adolescent boys;
- preexisting emotional difficulties;
- preexisting conflict between the child and the deceased;
- a surviving parent who becomes excessively dependent on the child;
- lack of adequate family or community supports, or a parent who cannot use support systems;
- unstable, disrupted environments, including numerous caretakers and broken routines;
- a parent who marries someone with whom the child has a bad relationship;
- sudden or violent death (including suicide or murder).

Because children are dependent, their well-being is tied to parent and family support and functioning. A child's reaction to adversity and trauma is highly influenced by the parents' or caregivers' responses and the quality of caregiving the child receives following the event(s). Children have a difficult time dealing effectively with trauma if parents are highly distressed and unable to provide support and adequate care. Children often need extra attention and nurturing and to trust that their experience and reactions are accepted and understood. Parents and other family members, struggling with their own traumatic distress, may be unable to provide a structured, supportive, and regulated response for their children. If family functioning, such as structure, routine, and organization, is disrupted or chaotic, children have a more difficult time.

One important subset of families who have been traumatized is those with at least one member who is suffering from PTSD. PTSD is the most common disorder resulting from exposure to trauma. This disorder is characterized by a set of symptoms that include, but are not limited to: experiencing recurrent nightmares, intrusive thoughts, or flashbacks of a traumatic event; generalized apathy, numbing, or negative emotional state; avoidance of thoughts, persons, or places associated with a traumatic event; hypervigilance; and other symptoms of increased arousal lasting longer than one month (American Psychiatric Association, 1994). Some victims experience bouts of amnesia or difficulty remembering the details of what happened surrounding the traumatizing experiences or catastrophes.

In the acute phase of PTSD, symptoms associated with anxiety tend to predominate, as do startle responses, intrusive thoughts, flashbacks of the incident, and sleep problems. Sometimes PTSD sufferers recover, in part with the help of social supporters, particularly family members. However, some PTSD cases either become delayed in onset or are chronic. Here the symptoms become more problematic. Clients who develop chronic PTSD tend also to display symptoms of depression and despondency, somatic symptoms, and, for some, irritable, angry, and aggressive tendencies.

As we have indicated previously, age and stage of development influence how the hallmark symptoms of PTSD are expressed. For your reference, in Table 2.2 we list common symptoms of PTSD and indicate the age group in which they are most often exhibited.

If multiple individuals within the family are coping with trauma, even if everyone was exposed to the same event at the same time, no two reactions will be the same. One individual may react immediately, showing distress from the moment the traumatic event begins. Another individual may not exhibit signs of traumatic distress for days, weeks, or even months following the onset. One individual may become irritable and have frequent angry outbursts, while another individual has crying spells and an unremitting sadness. Some family members may not be symptomatic at all. The family trauma clinician who

**TABLE 2.2.** Summary of Common Victim Reactions by Age Grouping

|  | Pre-school | School Age | Teens | Adults |
|---|---|---|---|---|
| Changes in play/posttraumatic play | X | X |  |  |
| Trauma-related/new fears and worries | X | X | X | X |
| Separation anxiety | X | X |  |  |
| Distress at reminders | X | X | X | X |
| Sleep disturbances | X | X | X | X |
| Somatic complaints | X | X | X | X |
| Developmental regression | X | X |  |  |
| Acting out, irritability, aggression | X | X | X | X |
| Withdrawal | X | X | X | X |
| Sadness, depression | X | X | X | X |
| Difficulties with attention, concentration, memory | X | X | X | X |
| Exaggerated startle | X |  |  |  |
| Hypervigilance | X | X | X | X |
| School phobias and other school problems |  | X | X |  |
| Flashbacks |  |  | X | X |
| Interpersonal problems |  | X | X | X |

understands that individuals show a range of responses to experiences of trauma will be prepared to deal with the complexities this creates.

## The Trauma Response From a Developmental Life Span Perspective

Families are made up of individuals spanning multiple ages and developmental stages. Working with a family that has been exposed to trauma, the clinician must recognize that trauma can and will have differing effects depending on the age of individual members. In other words, young children will react differently than adolescents; adolescents will react differently than adults. Taking a developmental life span perspective is necessary to understand the trauma response of individual family members.

Children and adolescents have different reactions to trauma depending on their cognitive and psychosocial development. Their capacity to appraise traumatic situations and their available coping strategies determine how they will respond (Compas et al., 2001). Working effectively with children who have been traumatized, even within the context of helping and empowering their families, requires a clear understanding of child development and the typical methods children use to cope with stress, particularly traumatic stress.

Victims of childhood trauma experience a complex set of physiological, emotional, cognitive, and behavioral reactions that occur both during and after the traumatic event(s) and, because development is occurring rapidly across all of these domains, viewing trauma within a developmental context is no easy task (M. R. Harvey & Herman, 1994; Herman, 1986). Young children's emerging capacities influence everything from (1) the types of trauma they are likely to experience, (2) their appraisal of the traumatic event, and (3) the impact of the trauma (as a result of differences in the forms of symptom expression and of the coping skills available to children at particular stages of development) to (4) their ability to join their family in collaborative coping or to make use of specific therapeutic techniques to aid recovery (see Loman, Gunnar, & the Early Experience, Stress and Neurodevelopment Center Team, 2010; National Scientific Council on the Developing Child, 2005).

## Response From a Developmental Life Span Perspective

Understanding the reactions of children to trauma necessitates a clear grasp of their developmental competencies around the time of the trauma and the potential for trauma to interfere with their expected developmental trajectory. The family trauma clinician needs to carefully consider (1) what developmental skills and abilities a child has for appraising a traumatic event, (2) the impact of development on the child's traumatic response both during and after the traumatic event, and (3) the potential impact of trauma on the developmental trajectory in both the short and long term.

## Family's Role as Natural Healer

Only a small minority of children and adults who are traumatized by various events actually see a psychotherapist. Most recover without professional assistance. For children, the way adults attend to them is important for positive adaptation. Children exposed to frightening stressors, for example, require the calming and protective presence of a parent. This sensitive adult is able to get the child to articulate the source of her or his anxiety and all of the associated fears.

For the most part, families are in effect social contexts for managing the stress of their members. We note that families usually possess the capacity for coping with a wide variety of stressors. By listening carefully to what family members say and feel and feeding this information back to them, families are able to help their members work through most of their traumatic experiences. Moreover, they are able to learn from their experiences so that they will feel more competent and confident about future challenges.

Indeed, as an intimate social support system, family members promote recovery in at least four separate and related ways: (1) detecting traumatic stress, (2) ensuring safety, (3) giving family members permission to talk about what happened, and (4) supporting positive adaptations.

## Detecting Traumatic Stress

The first way families help is simply by caring enough to notice. Traumatic stress is usually first detected in families because family members know one another so well; they can notice any changes in emotion and behavior. The word "family" is derived from the Latin term *familia*. It is the root word of "familiar" and literally means "household." Unlike in modern Western cultures, in earlier times a household often included many people.

Anyone bound by a household—be they tied by blood or law or choice— becomes well aware of the habits, dispositions, and patterns of behavior of fellow inhabitants. Add to this the similarities of inherited and acquired traits of family members, and what emerges in most families is a remarkable "feel" for the normative behavior of fellow family members.

Thus, in a "healthy" family, when one family member is having a "bad" day, other family members know it immediately. When a family member has experienced a catastrophe, he or she is expected to behave differently. Even when a family member displays symptoms of PTSD for which the cause may be unknown, other family members detect the changed pattern of behavior almost immediately.

Once a member's stress reactions are noticed, family members are also in a position to begin to help the stressed family member. Family members help each other face the cause of the behavior, most often the stressor or traumatic experiences. This may be done by simply linking the apparent stress reaction to some recent event. The way this link is made is most often tailored to the individual needs and style of the victim in a way that only another family member could know.

A couple of case examples illustrate how families use some fairly common therapeutic strategies for helping their loved ones make this link. Jimmy's parents noticed some changes in his behavior: apathy and preoccupation. They asked Jimmy what was wrong but received only genuine denials. Still concerned, Jimmy's mother baked his favorite pie and, away from everyone else, said: "James Roberts, I know there's something eating inside you, and I think I know what it is [she did not], but I want you to tell me yourself right now. And you're not leaving until you do." Jimmy then told his mother about the death of a pen pal and about his dreams and thoughts of ending his own life like his friend of many years. His mother's approach would never work with some children, but it did with Jimmy.

For other family members, a more subtle method has proven more effective over the years. In the case of the Murray family, for example, long before they sought help from a professional psychotherapist Mrs. Murray left Mr. Murray a copy of a book about Vietnam veterans' readjustment problems after he had a week of nightmares about the war. He had responded favorably in the past to receiving from her various books and articles about problems he was facing at the time.

In some families, though, recognizing that a family member is distressed as a result of a traumatic experience does not happen so easily or automatically. For instance, parents often have a difficult time attributing their child's distress to traumatic events. They may see their child's difficulty as related to other common childhood emotional or behavioral problems, such as attention deficit hyperactivity disorder or oppositional defiant disorder. They may feel guilty for failing to protect their child from a trauma and want to believe that their child is not damaged (even temporarily) as a result. Making the link between trauma and distress symptoms may need to be addressed early in a therapeutic encounter. We will discuss this further in the next chapter.

## Ensuring Safety

A normal part of the "righting response" for a family following the experience of trauma is increasing protection. Family members are likely to be more solicitous of each other. Parents are likely to increase supervision and monitoring. They often introduce more structure to their daily routines. Family members tend to want to spend more time together and they also tend to communicate more frequently with each other when not together.

In qualitative research on changes in families following trauma, the theme of increased protection emerged (Kiser, Nurse, Luckstead, & Collins, 2008). Caregivers indicated that their whole family was more watchful and concerned about each other's well-being. One caregiver stated:

> The boys got closer with her [their sister after she was hit by a car].... They were really worried about her. No matter how much they argued they was still worried, scared. And her and the younger son, they started to get closer and played together. It was like he was watching over her, protecting her and made sure when they went across the street she was holding his hand and stuff. (Kiser et al., 2008, p. 83)

## Giving Family Members Permission to Talk About What Happened

A third way that families provide social support and facilitate recovery from trauma is helping the traumatized member reconsider the traumatic events: to recapitulate what happened. Talking to others about what happened is an important part of the healing process for most trauma victims. Who better to share with than a family member who is already privy to one's intimate thoughts and feelings?

---

### Associated Skill

Family Storytelling. Families tell each other stories. These stories are used to share experiences (both the best and the worst of lived experience), to put these experiences into a shared context, to pass along important messages, and to define the family's past, present, and future. As families share stories, they practice the skills of telling and listening. As narrators, family members decide what to tell, how much detail to provide, and with what emotional overlay. As listeners, family members practice taking different perspectives and accepting both the facts and the emotions as part of the orator's reality. Family storytelling goes beyond telling and listening; it involves a coordinated perspective (Bohanek, Marin, Fivush, & Duke, 2006), collaborative problem-solving (Berg et al., 1998), co-regulation of affect, and a joint frame (Hill, Fonagy, Safier, & Sargent, 2003). Family storytelling provides an important skill base for helping individuals share their trauma memories.

---

Family members can listen to a trauma story over and over again and help the trauma survivor answer five fundamental questions: (1) What happened? (2) Why did it happen? (3) Why did I and others act as we did then? (4) Why did I and others act as we did since then? (5) If something like this happened again, would I be able to cope more effectively? In the process of telling about what happened, the family member enables the survivor to clarify insights as she or he recalls facets of the trauma that are critical in answering these questions. All five of the victim questions must be answered to the satisfaction of the victim.

## Knowing and Understanding What Happened

The fourth way families support family members who have been traumatized is in helping the victim work through her or his traumatic memories and accompanying conflicts. Recovering from traumatic stress is the process of developing more effective methods of memory management. With regard to this skill, families enable fellow members to more effectively "manage" their memories by correcting one member's distorted views or conclusions in a way that will lead to effective recovery. In the course of treatment a family client of mine (CRF) related a story about when her mother began to recall being sexually molested by her uncle as a young girl. First her husband and then her older daughter urged her to relate the painful story. Both helped her to admit that, although she had felt guilty and partially responsible for the molestation for the past quarter-century, she had been an innocent, unsuspecting child, and that her uncle had committed a crime.

---

### Associated Skill

Correcting Distortions. Well-functioning families are able to gently guide a fellow family member to view various situations from a different perspective (e.g., to place blame and credit more objectively). This is a part of what could be called basic family relations skills (Figley & McCubbin, 1983; Guerney, 1982). Often parents show, for example, an extraordinary capacity to help their children sort out blame and credit for their actions. This may be due in part to some parents spending more time with their children, knowing them better, and working at it more diligently.

---

Most importantly, families help victims by "reframing" or offering alternative ways of viewing the highly stressful event and the event-related consequences in a more positive or optimistic way. For example, the traumatic event was "God's test of our faith" or "it made us more aware of how other victims feel." In this way, families help the victim formulate a "healing theory" (Figley, 1979, 1998). The family serves as an effective facilitator in developing a healing theory of the entire experience, a reframing of the predicament.

## Associated Skills

Clarifying Insights. Family members often have the ability to accurately understand a member's perspective and, in turn, explain it to him or her. This skill involves family members in listening carefully to another's views or insights in a nonjudgmental and caring manner, and then succinctly paraphrasing these views for the family member in a way that demonstrates both understanding of the facts and acceptance of the feelings. In studies of successful families (Figley, 1985a, 1986; Figley & McCubbin, 1983; H. McCubbin & Figley, 1983b) we found that family members were effective in helping family members, including those most troubled by highly stressful events, to clarify insights, perspectives, frameworks, and discoveries about their ordeal. Moreover, family members then would refer to these clarifications later as they relate to constructing a healing theory or reframing some aspect of their experiences.

Supporting Reframes. Similarly, family members often have the ability to offer or support new and more "generous" or accurate perspectives on the impairing stress reactions (Figley, 1983). This change in perspective can involve, for example, positively connoting what has previously been viewed as negative. These new perspectives are the final major building blocks for constructing a healing theory for the family and are thus critical skills for effectively helping family members work through their traumatic experiences (Figley, 1988c).

Developing such a healing theory requires considerable knowledge about the victim. Such knowledge is well known to fellow family members but is acquired very slowly by therapists or others attempting to assist the victim. Family members, for example, may know best whether to be active or passive, use mutual self-disclosure or not, or be confrontational or not. As will be discussed in Chapter seven, we partner with client families either to activate or to develop these same naturally occurring family social supportiveness skills in therapy.

## Professional Help for Individuals With PTSD and Other Stress-Related Disorders

At the same time, there may be a point in the recovery process where some families get "stuck" in the process of helping an individual family member cope with traumatic distress. They are unable to effectively utilize the information they have about the trauma and its consequences in order to resolve or eliminate the traumatic stress.

For those who do not recover, we know how to help. Certainly, PTSD has now received the necessary scientific attention to support development of effective, verifiable, and replicable treatment methods. Practice guidelines for PTSD are now available (American Psychological Association, 2004; Cohen et al., 2010; Foa, Keane, Friedman, & Cohen, 2008; VA/DoD Clinical Practice Guideline Working Group, 2003). These guidelines provide expert advice on screening, assessment, and treatment for children, adolescents, and adults who meet the criteria for full or partial PTSD. We will summarize the best practices in use today.

Again, working effectively with individuals who have been traumatized requires a clear understanding of child development, typical methods individuals use to cope with traumatic and posttraumatic stress, and the circumstances of the traumatizing and recovering context.

Evaluation of traumatic stress disorders requires assessment of traumatic experiences and of related symptoms. Multiple checklists are available for recording an individual's exposure to traumatic events. Many ask about exposure to a variety of trauma types (sexual abuse, accidents, medical trauma, interpersonal violence, disaster) and include additional questions to determine whether the exposure meets the current diagnostic criteria for a trauma.

There are a variety of well-developed tools[1] to assess the trauma-related symptoms in adults. The most commonly used by clinicians are the PTSD Checklist (PCL) and the Clinician Administered PTSD Scale (CAPS). Standardized instruments are also available for evaluating PTSD symptoms in children and adolescents. For young children, parent-report of symptoms on instruments such as the Trauma Symptom Checklist for Young Children (TSCYC) can be helpful. For children, starting around eight years of age, self-report measures such as the UCLA PTSD Index for DSM-IV are appropriate. A version of the UCLA PTSD Index captures the same information from parents, who often have a different perspective on their child's distress. A child version of the CAPS is also available (Clinician Administered PTSD Scale for Children [CAPS-CA]) and is helpful for clinicians who feel that a more formal clinical assessment is needed. Assessment of co-occurring emotional and behavioral problems is also recommended.

Individuals who meet either partial or full diagnostic criteria for PTSD will benefit from trauma-focused treatment. Consistent with our own thinking, the literature provides support for some core intervention objectives for helping individuals with traumatic stress disorders:

1  assuring the individual's safety, which includes preventing re-exposure or re-victimization;
2  identifying and regulating the expression of emotions such as anger, grief, fear, guilt, and self-blame;
3  learning new skills for coping;
4  processing the trauma by (a) helping face the truth of what has happened and (b) dealing with misperceptions and cognitive distortions, such as the "damaged goods syndrome"—poor self-image, avoidance of interpersonal relations, and so on;
5  helping identify and access supportive resources—for example, who can he or she trust, and how can he or she protect him- or herself in the future?

The literature provides support for some additional intervention objectives with childhood trauma:

6  returning to a normal developmental trajectory;
7  renewing a sense of mastery and positive meaning.

Specific trauma-focused treatments have proven effectiveness for helping children, adolescents, and adults. Research generally affirms the effectiveness of phased approaches that include the following intervention strategies: psycho-education, anxiety management training, affect regulation skill development, and cognitive therapy followed by direct exploration of the traumatic experience with exposure/contingency reinforcement programs, evaluation and reframing of cognitions, and support (Cloitre, Koenen, Cohen, & Han, 2002).

Trauma-focused cognitive behavior therapy (CBT) is typically the treatment of choice (Forbes et al., 2010; Friedman, Resick, & Keane, 2007). For adults, prolonged exposure, cognitive processing therapy, group CBT, and eye movement desensitization and reprocessing (EMDR), all of which may be considered CBT approaches, receive first-level ratings in practice guidelines. For children and adolescents, trauma-focused CBT (T-F CBT) is the most widely studied and used treatment. Importantly, parent participation in T-F CBT has been shown to improve child outcomes. Cognitive behavioral intervention for trauma in schools (CBITS) is a group intervention designed to be implemented in school settings, where it has the potential for reaching significant numbers of children with trauma-related disorders. For children under the age of six years, child–parent psychotherapy (CPP), which focuses on improving the parent–child relationship, is an effective model. New promising treatment approaches are also being developed and evaluated.

## Note

1  All assessments noted here can be requested through the National Center for PTSD of the Department of Veterans Affairs, http://www.ptsd.va. gov/index.asp

# three

# Spreading Beyond the Individual

## Family Adaptation to Stress and Trauma

Families operate as systems and, as such, something that effects one member creates a reaction in other family members, dyadic subsystems, and the family unit. Through a variety of mechanisms, stressful and traumatic experiences impact the family. In this chapter we begin to share our understanding about families as dynamic systems with interpersonal connectivity. We will discuss various formal and informal family routines and rituals of daily living; we will also explore the ways in which routines are disrupted by adversity. Additionally, we will discuss the ways in which families work together to control and manage more effectively the unwanted impact of the trauma. We illustrate the concept of a family system by discussing a variety of family processes within a systemic framework. We will look at the ways in which exposure to trauma impacts family subsystems and the family as a whole (Collins et al., 2010; Kiser & Black, 2005). We will use this information to suggest a model of family adaptation to trauma. This model will allow us to build a comprehensive intervention strategy for helping families impacted by trauma.

## Cost of Caring

Families can provide valuable support and assistance to vulnerable family members, but there is also a cost to caring. I have noted elsewhere (Figley, 1982, 1983, 1988a, 1995, 2002a) that there are costs to providing social support, particularly for close family members. Indeed, as catastrophes affect individuals, so do they affect the families of these victims: such families should be viewed as the "families of catastrophe."

One of the costs of caring is that, as family members attend to the pain and suffering of their loved ones, they feel pain and suffer too (Burgess & Holmstron, 1979; Figley, 1982, 1983, 1985b, 1988c). This is not unlike the phenomenon of couvade, in which expectant fathers simulate the symptoms and experiences of their pregnant wives to the extent that their abdomens become swollen and they complain of diarrhea and vomiting in the absence of medical causes (see Rabkin & Struening, 1976). Psychosomatic medicine has reported similar phenomena: entire families developing various maladies directly associated with some family-centered upheaval such as residential mobility (Mann, 1972) or divorce (Hetherington, Cox, & Cox, 1976).

An incident in our (CRF) household may provide a simple example of the cost of caring. Our eleven-year-old daughter, Jessica, had accidentally washed one of her contact lenses down the drain. Though not the end of the world as we know it, this was a stressful event for Jessica. For months she had looked forward to dumping her nerdy, oversized glasses in favor of contacts. She was screaming from the other room, "*Dad!* I can't find my contact!" As I tried unsuccessfully to retrieve the lens and it became clear that it was lost, she began to cry. The crying quickly increased, and soon our three-year-old, Laura, began to cry, saying, "I'm so sad for my sister," sob, sob, "cause I love my sister."

In addition to being directly affected by catastrophes as individuals, persons belonging to families with a victimized member may experience traumatic stress.

Family members may be traumatized in at least four separate ways:

1. **simultaneous effects**, as when catastrophe directly strikes the entire family (for example, fire, natural disaster, auto accident);
2. **vicarious effects**, as when a catastrophe strikes one family member with whom the family is unable to make direct contact (for example, war, coal mine accident);
3. **chiasmal effects**, as when the traumatic stress appears to "infect" other family members after they make contact with the victimized member (for example, a nightmare about snakes after a family member discloses almost being bitten by one); and
4. **intrafamilial trauma**, as when a catastrophe strikes from within the family (for example, incest, violence, divorce).

## Simultaneous Effects

This is when families experience a traumatic event all at the same time. It could mean enduring a natural disaster, such as a tornado or earthquake (Litz, 2004; Walsh, 2007).

Perhaps one of the reasons why natural disasters appear so disruptive is that they often strike intact social support systems such as families, neighborhoods, and communities simultaneously. Conversely, this widespread destruction is linked with considerable social and emotional disruption (Gleser, Green, & Winget, 1981).

Though less studied, families also experience trauma simultaneously as a result of human causes such as car accidents, residential fires, and criminal assault. As a result, *everyone* is a fellow survivor and is able to appreciate and provide effective and knowledgeable support. There is little "blaming the victim," for example, because everyone in the family is a victim. Families affected simultaneously by disaster are able to help each other to overcome the emotional horrors, to rebuild, and to recognize any valuable lessons that can be learned. Catastrophe-related pathology is less frequent in these situations than in the others.

## Vicarious Effects

In contrast, when we learn by some medium (for example, telephone, television, letter, Facebook, or Twitter) that a catastrophe has affected someone we love, this is extremely stressful (Figley, 1982, 1983; Walsh, 2007), and recovery can take years. The emotional attachments of family and friendship enable us to feel safe, secure, and loved (Figley, 1973; H. McCubbin & Figley, 1983a; Norris, Byrne, Diaz, & Kaniasty, 2001). The experience of a large group of Americans held hostage in Iran provides an illustration of this phenomenon (Figley, 1980; Figley & McCubbin, 1983): the hostages' families at home experienced more stress than many of the hostages. For example, while the daily routine of the hostages was highly regimented and predictable, with little access to new information, the hostages' families were constantly bombarded with new information about the captivity experience (most often false rumors), and their routine constantly changed. Frequently, families of hostages were forced to respond to a wide variety of new situations they neither welcomed nor were prepared to deal with.

## Chiasmal Effects: "Infecting" the Family With Trauma

In the process of attending to the victimization of a family member, supportive family members themselves are touched emotionally, albeit indirectly. They are affected by the reactions of the victimized family member through their efforts to help. Figley (1983) has described this phenomenon as secondary catastrophic stress response. Others have used other terms to describe this and similar responses.

A study by Kishur and Figley (1987) has presented evidence of this phenomenon long observed in the clinical literature. They describe the phenomenon of the "transmission" of behaviors in general and emotional experiences in particular as the chiasmal effects of traumatic stressors. Specifically, they define it as "the phenomenon of behaviors, impressions, actions, attitudes, or emotions which are first seen in one person following an emotionally traumatic event and subsequently observed in a supporter at a later time" (p. 3).

In their study of crime victims and their supporters—especially family members—Kishur and Figley (1987) noted that:

> as expected, the major predictor of *supporter distress was victim distress* [and] it is clear that a pattern of effects emerged in both the victim and supporter. The crime victims as well as their supporters suffered from the crime episode long after the initial crisis had passed. Symptoms of depression, social isolation, disruptions of daily routine, and suspicious feelings of persecution affected the lives of these persons. (p. 18)

Thus, in the process of abating posttraumatic stress reactions, supporters are quite susceptible to being traumatized themselves. It is especially important, therefore, that each person who appears to be suffering from posttraumatic stress reactions be viewed within a family context of those victimized indirectly as a result of their concern for the victim.

As researchers—and as human beings—we clinicians often attend too much to those directly exposed to traumatic events. Those who care about these "victims" are rarely acknowledged as also being victims, as suffering from the same extraordinary stressors and as struggling to put their lives back together.

Our approach to treating traumatized families recognizes these struggles. In our work with families we try to assist each member to face and eliminate any unwanted consequences of stressors and to do it with minimal cost to other family members.

Yet there are some traumatic events or situations that are particularly difficult to prevent and treat. This is certainly true for intrafamily trauma.

## Intrafamily Trauma

Families certainly have the capacity to be extremely helpful in enabling family members in recovering from traumatic stressors. They may become traumatized through their assistance. They may also be traumatized from the abuse of other family members.

It is well established in the research and treatment literature that families can be the context for victimization. Between 1993 and 2004, intimate partner violence on average made up 22% of nonfatal intimate partner victimizations against women. The same year, intimate partners committed 3% of all violent crime against men (Catalano, 2007).

Family violence and abuse have probably always been a major health problem, and public awareness of this problem in the past two decades has led to major legislation and policies for protection from this form of abuse. Families traumatized from intrafamily abuse are often the most difficult to detect and treat. This is due primarily to the difficulty in establishing mutual trust, commitment, and supportiveness between the victim(s) and victimizer(s). Recent disturbing statistics regarding children suffering from child abuse and neglect show that over 3 million reports of child abuse are made every year. In 2009 this was 3.3 million reports, involving 6 million children (U.S. Department of Health and Human Services, Administration for Children and Families, Administration on Children, Youth and Families, & Children's Bureau, 2010).

## The Family's Systemic Responses

Within families relational processes are central to the functioning of the family. Relational processes occur between and among individual family members. As family members interact with each other over time and in specific roles, dyadic (or multipartite) subsystems form. These subsystems include the adult partnerships, the parenting or caregiving subsystem, parent–child subsystems, and the sibling subsystem. According to systems theory, each of these subsystems must work together effectively for the family unit to function effectively.

Research demonstrates however, that relational processes are impacted by trauma and that this can alter the functioning of multiple subsystems within the family. From our experience working with families who have been traumatized, the dynamics of dyadic and multipartite relational processes add complexity to family treatment and must be carefully considered. We will briefly explore the most common effects seen in each subsystem (Collins et al., 2010; Kiser & Black, 2005).

## Dyadic or Relational Responses to Trauma

### Adult Partnerships

As any family therapist knows, in most two-parent families, the couple's relationship is often the anchor for the family. Within a healthy partnership, this relationship serves as a source of support and strength when faced with trauma. However, if the couple cannot communicate about or agree on what happened, why it happened, or how to handle it, their interactions often become conflicted and blaming. These negative interactions can lead to an increased risk of interpersonal violence or separation/divorce (Felson & Outlaw, 2007).

### Parenting and Parent–Child Relationships

There is clear evidence now that the experience of trauma by either a parent or child or both alters parenting and parent–child relationships. Parenting even under normal conditions requires considerable energy, effort, and emotional resources. Under conditions of high stress, many parents cannot mobilize these resources and their parenting suffers (Ceballo & McLoyd, 2002; Conger et al., 2002; Pinderhughes, Nix, Foster, & Jones, 2001; Repetti & Wood, 1997). Parents may not be able to respond to their children with as much warmth and sensitivity. They may not be as attentive and supportive. They may overreact and use more harsh and negative discipline.

If a parent is actually suffering from PTSD, his or her specific symptoms may interfere with taking care of the children (Appleyard & Osofsky, 2003; Scheeringa & Zeanah, 2001). Talking together about the trauma is more difficult if a parent is experiencing avoidance or is having difficulty remembering details about the trauma (Haden, 1998; Laible & Thompson, 2000). Managing daily family life is more difficult if parents are not sleeping well, suffering from depression, or having flashbacks.

The experience of trauma, especially interpersonal violence, which includes domestic violence and child abuse, fundamentally changes parent–child relationships. Attachment relationships are based on a sense of safety and protection that is irreparably harmed when these types of trauma occur within a family. In such situations, parents have not been able to provide protection, and relationships become more fragile, characterized by inconsistency and mistrust (Cook et al., 2005; Donnelly & Amaya-Jackson, 2002; Gagne & Bouchard, 2004).

### Sibling Subsystem

Siblings' interactions within the family are also reactive to stress and trauma. Children may find support from one another and by playing and talking together sort out some of their distressing thoughts and feelings. Sibling relationships, however, are closely tied to parental dynamics including preferential treatment of siblings and management of sibling conflict, including horizontal violence among siblings (Finkelhor, Ormrod, Turner, & Hamby, 2005).

The sibling subsystem is especially vulnerable and also potentially critical to recovery in situations where the traumatic events result in the siblings being placed outside the home and away from their parents. Consider, for example, the enormous role that the sibling subsystem plays for children who have witnessed extensive domestic violence culminating in the death of one parent and incarceration of the other. Having lost both parents, the children together must now carry their shared family history into a newly formed family unit.

As the various subsystems within the family make adjustments to deal with a trauma, the family unit is also impacted.

## Family Unit Responses to Trauma

Among the first efforts to recognize the role of social relationships in traumatic stress was Hill's (1949) classical study of the families of World War II veterans. Most observers consider Hill to have originated the concept of family stress. He was the first to suggest that the system of the family is greatly affected by crisis events such as war and postwar reunion. This sociological orientation emerged into what was later to be called the ABCX model of family crisis (Hill, 1949; Hill & Hansen, 1965) and has evolved into the current double ABCX model (H. McCubbin et al., 1980) and subsequent models (M. A. McCubbin & Patterson, 1983; Montgomery, 1982).

The Murray family and all families are fascinating systems, and, like the people who compose them, no two families are alike. To understand the best ways of helping families impacted by trauma, indeed any family, is to appreciate the "healing" or ameliorative potential of the system—that there is a range of coping abilities, strengths, and resource reserves in all families to recover. Our job as family specialists is to discover our family client's natural resources and what they need to mobilize these resources and manage their challenges effectively.

As we noted earlier, the human body is a self-contained system able to recover from a wide variety of ailments and physical traumas, and the family system has similar capabilities. As members of a family we come to rely on one another in the family to perform certain functions at a certain minimum level of competence under certain conditions.

For the Murray family, for example, both parents work and provide shelter, income, and protection for themselves and their children. Moreover, the parents are responsible for the reproduction, nurturance, education, and socialization of their children. The spouses rely on each other for love, companionship, friendship, sexual gratification, and general social support. The children are a source of love, encouragement, and stimulation (that is, they drive you crazy sometimes!). With so many important functions being performed by so few people, it is not surprising that we are so affected and influenced by other members of our family. It is also why families are such an extraordinary source of stress production and reduction (Figley, 1983, 1988c).

## Model of Family Adaptation to Trauma

The extensive research and scholarly literature about the traumatized more often focuses on explaining how individuals deal with trauma than explaining how families deal with trauma. Among the goals of this book is to provide tools for understanding and helping families. With that in mind we offer the Family Adaptation to Trauma Model (Figure 3.1), which attempts to illustrate how families manage current stressors, including traumatic stressors, and how to view their ability to adapt on a continuum of Thriving, to Maintaining, to Struggling, and then to Failing. What is different than with earlier models, however, is that we view the adaptation to trauma in more *systemic* terms. Specifically, we believe that adaptation is a continual process that can either help or hinder current and future family functioning but most often does both.

To explain the model briefly, consider a family who have experienced a traumatic event. In trying to understand how families may respond to the trauma, *Family Stress Reaction*, we must go beyond understanding the causes and consequences for that one trauma and consider all the other stressors or the *Current Stressor Context* affecting the family and its members. The effectiveness with which the family manage these family stressors—traumatic or otherwise—is a direct consequence of the *Family's Perceptions* or appraisal as a result of their "processing" or discussing and thinking through their situation and the availability of skills and methods for healing, the *Family's Healing Resources*. This process leads to adaptation. The family must find a new way of being, thinking, feeling, and doing consistent with their altered circumstances.

We define *Family Stress Reaction* as *the responses made by the family to the traumatic situation*. These responses are typically associated with resource utilization (family, friends, savings), co-regulation attempts (diminishing threats, prayer, rituals, distractions, routine), and developing shared meaning (framing, reframing, coming to an understanding, and perhaps a healing theory).

The *Family Stress Reaction* depends on three interdependent factors: the current stressor context; the perceptions about the stressors held by family members, particularly those in the most powerful and influential positions within the family; and the family's healing resources.

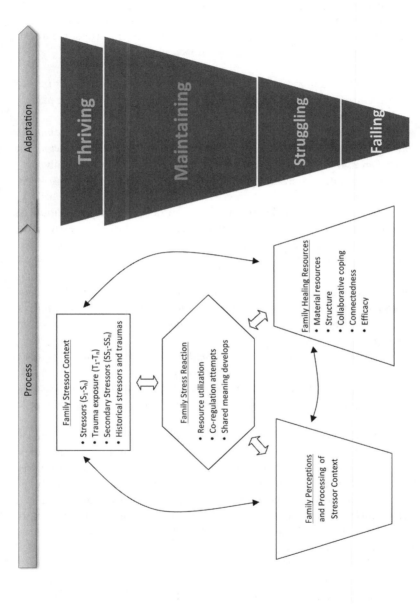

**FIGURE 3.1.** A Model of Family Adaptation to Trauma

The *Family Stressor Context* is defined as the *accumulation of stressors and strains placed on the family system during and following the traumatic event.* These stressors can include the traumatic event ($T1$) and its associated hardships ($SS1$), and also normative transitions, prior unresolved strains, and consequences of the family's efforts to cope. The current stressor context comprises stressors and traumas that are impacting the family.

- A stressor ($S$) is defined as an *event or series of events that demands immediate attention to control.* The stressor might be financial problems or having a new baby and may or may not cause a crisis for the family.
- A family traumatic event ($T1$) is defined as *an event that places the family or any one of its members in some kind of danger of physical, sexual, or psychological harm.* Over the course of the family life cycle the family may experience multiple traumas ($T2$, $T3$ . . . $Tn$). The family's reaction to each is influenced by their previous experience.
- Secondary stressors related to the trauma (for example, living in temporary housing for families who have suffered the loss of their home) may be limited to a few or may be a large number of quite serious threats to the family ($SS1$, $SS2$ . . . $SSn$).

*Family Perceptions and Processing* is defined as *the collective set of beliefs about the stressors that, in turn, lead to decisions about how to deal with the family's current context (the development and maintenance of an adaptation to the traumatic event and subsequent stressors).*

*Family Healing Resources* are *those tangible* (for example, material, economic) *and intangible* (for example, effective collaborative coping methods, cohesiveness, cooperativeness, and competence) *factors that are useful in solving problems related to recovering from the crisis and aftermath of the traumatic events.*

Adaptation can be reached at any one of a number of levels. At one end of the range is extremely good adaptation (Thriving), which means that the family not only coped well with the current trauma but also learned some valuable lessons; their coping repertoire has been enhanced through struggling with the current trauma. This positive adaptation leads to enhanced family healing resources during the current recovery process, which will enable the system to perceive future stressors as more manageable and prevent both future stressors and negative stress reactions.

At the other end of the continuum, however, the family can adapt poorly to the traumatic situation (Struggling/Failing). In many cases, families that are adapting poorly have chosen a strategy or tactic with short-term gains but long-term negative consequences. Use of drugs and alcohol to manage the stressful symptoms and the use of physical or psychological coercion to gain control are examples. These ineffective adaptive efforts result both in adding to the current list of stressors and in sowing the seeds for stressors that may emerge sometime in the future.

It is clear to us and many other practitioners that the volume in each segment of the triangle approximates the percentage of the population of families impacted by trauma in each level, with the "Maintaining" group being by far the largest group of families, with the "Thriving" group slightly ahead in numbers of those traumatized families who are in the "Struggling" group and who are in the "Failing" group. Certainly these proportions are influenced by socio-political and economic conditions which make families more or less vulnerable.

Is it possible to detect which families will be strengthened by traumatic events and which will not? Research from several decades by many scholars appears to indicate a dozen or so factors that tend to characterize families who adapt well (functional families) and those who adapt poorly to highly stressful events (dysfunctional families).

## Thriving/Maintaining

Just as individuals use coping strategies in the aftermath of traumatic events, so do families. Collaborative coping strategies important to families include, for example, negotiation, joint problem-solving, role clarity, understanding and balancing influence and control, and perspective taking (Berg et al., 1998; Figley, 1988b; M. A. McCubbin & McCubbin, 1993). Individual family members will have different skills relative to these collaborative coping strategies. Younger children will have limited problem-solving skills, and their ability to take the perspective of others will be just developing. Adults will and should wield more influence and control, and help scaffold the coping skills of younger members. Ultimately though, each family member contributes coping strengths that can promote adaptive coping when the family works together.

After decades of clinical practice and study with families, we are able to differentiate families who cope well with stress, even the stress associated with highly stressful events, from those who do not (Figley, 1983; H. McCubbin & Figley, 1983a; M. A. McCubbin & Patterson, 1983; Walsh, 2003). Families that are able to right themselves following trauma recognize their situation and respond rapidly, make creative and flexible use of their resources, communicate openly, and build consensus about the meaning of trauma. "The ability of many families to cope with and withstand daily hassles, critical transitions and cataclysmic events while maintaining their critical functions is a tribute to the vitality of the institution" (Kiser, Ostoja, & Pruitt, 1998, p. 102). We briefly describe the characteristics associated with families who either avoid or quickly recover from traumatic experiences:

- **Clear acceptance of stressor.** Effective families are able to quickly accept that their family is being forced to struggle with a highly stressful event or series of events. They may find themselves temporarily bewildered by over-whelming events but quickly recover and begin to mobilize their energy and resources for action.
- **Family-centered locus of problem.** Effective families quickly shift the focus of the problem or stressor away from any one family member or set of members and recognize it as a problem or challenge for the entire family. The Murray family, to their credit, quickly recognized that Tammy's depression was part of and, indeed, a result of the pileup of stressors impacting on everyone in the family, and that all of the stressors had to be addressed at some point.
- **Solution-oriented problem-solving.** Effective families get stuck only briefly on who is to blame for the current crisis or trauma and then move on to mobilize their resources to correct the situation together.
- **High tolerance.** Effective families' members tend to have even more toler-ance for each other during a highly stressful time than in times of relative calm. They tend to recognize the need for conciliation, patience, and consideration in times that require cooperation and teamwork.
- **Clear and direct expressions of commitment and affections.** Similarly, effective families tend to have members who are especially clear and direct about their feelings toward one another, particularly expressions of commit-ment to each other—irrespective of whether times are difficult or not. Moreover, effective families are generous with their praise and signs of affection, both verbal and nonverbal.
- **Open and effective communication.** Not only do members of effective families communicate with one another about affection and commitment, but they tend to have few sanctions against when and what to talk about and, indeed, enjoy talking with one another about a wide range of topics. They make sure that unresolved family conflicts do not interfere with adaptive coping.
- **High family cohesion.** Effective families have members who enjoy each other's company, miss each other when they are away, are proud to be part of the family, and speak with pride about each other. This cohesiveness is especially important when the family is traumatized, when they may need each other more than ever.
- **Flexible family roles.** All family members play many roles within their family: completing household chores, earning and consuming income, communicating with relatives and friends, and other tasks on behalf of the family. In effective families, these roles are often played by more than one person. This is especially important in times of crisis and trauma, when one or more members may be unable to function effectively. Families who can

quickly reorganize and re-establish functional roles are most successful at limiting traumatic distress.

- **Maintenance of structure and predictability.** Family life works in large part because of organization and routines that allow the family to accomplish all of the tasks that must get done every day. Being part of a family means knowing when and how things are done. Effective families make an effort to keep these routines in place so that family members can take comfort in some predictability and stability in their lives.
- **Efficient resource utilization.** Effective families are able to access their own resources (interpersonal, material) and those outside the family—either professional or nonprofessional—without difficulty and with little sense of embarrassment. Effective families allow each individual member to contribute to the solution. They are also able to recognize that under certain circumstances relying on others is especially important, since they would expect to provide similar services to their friends and kin when they are in need.
- **Belief in their ability to succeed.** Effective families trust their ability to cope with high stress and trauma. They set high expectations for themselves and, regardless of how bad the situation, they know they can mobilize the necessary resources to overcome the stress and trauma. They are appreciative and acknowledge the contributions of all family members. Effective families are also able to appreciate the opportunities that may be created by the challenges they face.
- **Shared meaning.** Effective families use their shared belief system to come to an understanding of the stressor that makes sense to them. Families frequently need all of their collaborative coping skills to accomplish this difficult and demanding task.

## Struggling/Failing

There are, of course, families who utilize dysfunctional coping methods in efforts to avert or ameliorate a traumatic situation. To a certain extent they are the reverse of the functional coping characteristics. Sometimes dysfunctional family coping is related to the maladaptive coping strategies used by individual family members. For example, although highly emotional outbursts, from screaming to weeping, are normal and expected responses to trauma, some families resort to violence when under considerable stress. Similarly, though adult family members may drink socially and use prescribed drugs, in dysfunctional families substances are used as a method of stress reduction. The use of violence or substances reduces the family's ability to successfully navigate the traumatic circumstances and often leads to maladaptation. In many instances, families who are struggling or failing are at high risk for dissolution. Under significant stress, relational bonds become weakened and sometimes break. Divorce, separation, or placement of children outside the home can result.

Although dysfunctional family coping can be successful in reducing stress in the short term, it often leads to negative changes in family functioning. This is especially true if family stress levels remain high or the family is re-exposed to traumatic circumstances. In such cases, many families fail to reorganize and rebuild purposeful routines. Without a solid structure, family life becomes chaotic and, often, crisis oriented. Without an organized, stable, and predictable daily schedule, family relations may become strained. Finally, dysfunctional family coping strategies can become coping styles changing the ways in which family members view each other, their family, and the world.

## Conclusion

In this chapter we have tried to emphasize that families are a valuable resource for helping members recover from highly stressful, traumatic experiences. Recognizing the natural capacity of the family system for self-regulation, self-correction, and recovery from catastrophes and less extraordinary stressors, in the remainder of the book we try to describe our orientation to helping families. It should be clear then, if it is not clear already, that we are in awe of the family system. Certainly, families are responsible for considerable human misery: incest, physical and psychological abuse, discouragement, depression, loneliness. Yet we have witnessed, as researchers, as therapists, and as family members, quite remarkable growth and healing that takes place within families. As we have tried to explain, it is based on the lessons learned by studying *functional* families—those most successful in adapting to trauma and recovering to become even more resilient, effective, and efficient in dealing with future adversities. Helping families who have been traumatized involves respecting their capacity to heal themselves and being sure that we promote and do not inhibit that natural capacity.

# Part two
# Empowering Families

four

# Foundations of the Empowerment Treatment Approach

You might ask at this point, "So, how *do* you help families dealing with terrible things that have happened to them?" Simply put, we try to create the most conducive therapeutic environment possible and attempt to empower the family to help themselves. In this chapter and the five to follow we describe how to do this.

Owing to the relational impacts of trauma, we strongly believe that working to empower families to adapt successfully is a powerful and effective approach to treatment. Further, we believe that families, rather than the individual, are the appropriate unit of intervention. This chapter lays the foundation for a model of systemic trauma treatment. It includes four broad topics: (1) the empirical/theoretical basis for the model; (2) core treatment objectives that derive from the empirical/theoretical foundation; (3) core family trauma treatment techniques; and (4) an overview of a phased treatment model.

## Theoretical Orientation: Building Blocks

Our approach to helping families who have been traumatized is theoretically driven and rests upon multiple theories and disciplines. We briefly summarize these theoretical contributions.

## Traumatic Stress Studies and Crisis Intervention Theory

More than any other area, traumatic stress (Figley, 1998; Figley & Nash, 2007; Harvey & Pauwels, 2000) and crisis intervention (Harris, 1991; Roberts, 2005) models have shaped our thinking about human systems reactions to extra-ordinary stress.

The study of traumatic stress has led to a sophisticated understanding of the individual neurophysiological and psychosocial mechanisms that constitute the trauma response and are responsible for the symptoms related to traumatic stress disorders. For example, we now understand that the life threat response involves intense, coordinated neuronal excitation of cognitive, affective, sensory, integrative, regulatory, neuroendocrine, and motor functions, creating memorial representations. Once tagged for later potentiation, both external and internal reminders of the life-threatening event reactivate these neuronal networks. This iterative process is potentially responsible for many of the symptoms associated with PTSD, underscoring the relevance of memory functions for adaptation (Perry & Pollard, 1998; Schwarz, McNally, & Yeh, 1998). Understanding this process has important implications for working with families to recreate and process their collective memories of the traumatic events that are causing distress.

Even with significant advances in our knowledge, this line of research is still unraveling the complicated and interconnected nature of the biological and behavioral factors related to our reactions to trauma. As we learn more about how this reaction works, we are better able to design treatments that effectively address these disorders.

Crisis intervention theory emerged from a social need that arose when families and communities were no longer reliable as a resource for helping people in emergencies. There are certainly many crisis intervention theorists who have made extremely important contributions, including Lindemann (1944), Caplan (1964), and Jacobson, Strickler, and Morley (1968). These pioneers demonstrated that there is a set of psychological characteristics common to survivors of a wide variety of crises, that survivors show predictable or identifiable stress reactions as they pass through various stages in the process of working through their traumatic experiences, and that personal and environmental factors play a significant role in how the survivor attempts to maintain a homeostatic balance (Harris, 1991; Roberts, 2005).

From traumatic stress and crisis intervention studies, models of family stress and crisis have been developed. These theories include family risk/protection models that demonstrate that trauma and high stress influence individual well-being, which in turn impacts family functioning (Conger et al., 2002; Patterson, 2002; Pinderhughes, Dodge, Bates, Pettit, & Zelli, 2000).

In addition to the negative impacts of exposure to catastrophic events, traumatic stress studies are now focusing on the potential for positive outcomes and growth. Through struggling to overcome the unwanted consequences of trauma, individuals and families can become stronger. A solid literature exists indicating that some individuals and families survive severe traumas and through the reflective processes necessary for coping with trauma enhance their capacity and skills for (1) developing intimate relationships, (2) increasing personal/family hardiness or resilience, and (3) constructing new meanings for events that enhance understanding or acceptance of these events and give new meaning to life and to future goals and expectations (Tedeschi & Calhoun, 2004). These new directions in research provide us with some hopeful and empowering messages for families.

## Systems Theory

As we have discussed previously, systems theory is the primary theoretical orientation for viewing the effects of trauma on the family (Bronfenbrenner, 1979; Gelles & Maynard, 1987; Howes, Cicchetti, Toth, & Rogosch, 2000; Patterson, 1991; Shochet & Dadds, 1997). As noted in Chapter one, by viewing the family as a system and individual members and their dyadic/multipartite relationships within the family as subsystems, psychotherapists develop inter-vention programs to ameliorate various presenting problems of both the individual and the family. The contributions of systems theory to under-standing a family's trauma response involve several central tenets of the theory: (1) Systems are complex; the separate parts of the system are connected and interdependent. The interactions and interrelations among separate parts create a whole (which cannot be reduced to its separate parts). As applied to family trauma, when a traumatic event occurs, even to one member of the family, the entire family system is affected. (2) All systems seek homeostasis. Systems operate most effectively and efficiently when in balance. Traumatic events disrupt this homeostasis and throw the entire system out of balance. (3) Systems must change to regain homeostasis as quickly as possible. When a family is thrown out of balance by threats or traumas, they quickly try to "right" themselves or try to regain balance.

Building on general systems theory, family systems and family resiliency theories seek to explain the interconnectedness of individual family members and family subsystems to better understand how their shared history, familial bonds and collaborative coping strategies support the family's functioning, as well as how family-level risk and protective factors impede or support their ability to perform essential family functions, such as nurturance, protection, stability, and cohesion (Carver, 1998; Delage, 2002; Hernandez, Gangsei, & Engstrom, 2007; Patterson, 2002).

Systems theorists have significantly influenced both diagnostic and treat-ment approaches for helping families. For example, Olson and his associates

(Olson, Russell, & Sprenkle, 1989; Olson, Sprenkle, & Russell, 1979; Russell & Olson, 1983) provide an extremely useful diagnostic methodology for families with their circumplex model. They utilize adaptability and cohesion as the key concepts in measuring and diagnosing family pathology. The circumplex model is among the most empirically grounded systems approaches. It is designed both to generate information about particular families and to organize that information into relevant treatment goals. The McMaster model is another example of a systemic model to explain family functioning and influence how we help families change. This model assesses effective problem-solving, communication, role performance, affective responsiveness, affective involvement, and behavior control as keys to optimal family functioning (Bishop, Epstein, & Baldwin, 1980). The strategic systemic treatment approaches of Haley (1973, 1976, 1984), Madanes (1984), the Mental Research Institute group (Fisch, Weakland, & Segal, 1982; Watzlawick, Beavin, & Jackson, 1967; Watzlawick, Weakland, & Fisch, 1974), and Fraser (1989) offer other methods for viewing and changing family systems and subsystems.

## Attachment Theory and Relationship Models

Stemming from the seminal works of John Bowlby and Mary Ainsworth, attachment theory is critical for understanding family relations. From an evolutionary perspective, attachment theory explains the role of early parent–child relationships in the survival of the very young immature organisms of our species. Attachment theorists explained how the early bond that develops between a caregiver and her infant supports a sense of security and safety such that the infant could learn, explore, and ultimately separate. They demonstrated that this stable, nurturing, and supportive relationship with a trusted adult is internalized and becomes the basis for the formation of healthy relationships later in life. They also determined the negative consequences of disturbed or disrupted caregiving early in life.

Extending attachment theories beyond the caregiver–child relationship, other family relationships and patterns of relating take on significance. In the same way that infants form a working model of relationships from their responsive and caring interactions with their primary caregiver, family members develop family relationship schemas through consistent interactions with one another. These schemas provide guidelines that stipulate how family members react and interact with each other and are also extended to how family members relate to others. Attachment theory is useful for understanding how family relations either promote or hinder family member efforts at co-regulation and support seeking necessary for coping with trauma (Cicchetti, Cummings, Greenberg, & Marvin, 1990; Toth, Maughan, Manly, Spagnola, & Cicchetti, 2002).

## Death and Dying Theory

Trauma work often entails dealing with significant loss, so our approach to helping families impacted by trauma is indebted to the general field of death and dying, also called "grief work," "bereavement theory," or more recently "traumatic grief." The work of Bowlby (1961, 1969, 1980), Parks (1964, 1972), and Raphael (1973, 1983) has suggested but not identified the direct link between traumatic stress and grief reactions and their subsequent treatments. Traumatic grief theorists now suggest that, when someone dies in a sudden, gruesome, or violent fashion, the survivor develops many of the symptoms of PTSD and that these symptoms interfere with the grieving process (see Rynearson, 2006).

## Cognitive, Social, and Behavioral Psychology

As psychologists and human development specialists, we are well versed in the principles of cognitive, social, and behavioral psychology. The basic propositions and assumptions in these areas shape or at least influence our conceptualization, methods of study, and treatment of families who have been traumatized. Certainly the two-factor learning theory suggested by Mowrer (1947, 1960), emerging from both classical Pavlovian conditioning and instrumental learning, is an important basic framework. Moreover, the experiments of Solomon and his associates (R. L. Solomon, Kamin, & Wynne, 1953; R. L. Solomon & Wynne, 1954) with aversive stimuli were the first to link experimentally induced avoidance behavior and phobia. The empirically derived propositions associated with the link between stress reduction and exposure to conditioned stimuli in the absence of an unconditioned stimulus (Mineka, 1979), implosion therapy, and systematic desensitization (Kazdin & Wilcoxin, 1976; Levis & Hare, 1977; Rimm & Masters, 1979) have been influential to our work with trauma. Social learning theory places our understanding of how we recognize and respond to cues and cope with experiences within a social and relational context (Bandura, 1989; Cahill & Foa, 2007; Monson & Friedman, 2006; Pynoos, Steinberg, & Piacentini, 1999).

Two other theories have been used to explain family reactions to pressures and stresses, including eco-developmental theories and resource theories.

Eco-transactional or eco-developmental theories are important to understanding family trauma because of their emphasis on the role of context (Hill et al., 2003; Kazak, 1989; Meyers, Varkey, & Aguirre, 2002). Individuals and their behavior must be considered within their environmental context. Usually the influence of context is considered to be stronger through proximity, so an individual's family carries significant influence on the individual. Families are also embedded in neighborhoods or communities which impact the ways families react and interact and consequently influence the individual (Bronfenbrenner, 1979).

Resources theories, which are consistent with Hill's ABCX model of family stress, emphasize the role of resource loss in stress reactions (Hobfoll, 1988, 1989; Hobfoll & Lilly, 1993; Hobfoll, Lilly, & Jackson, 1992; Johnson, Palmieri, Jackson, & Hobfoll, 2007). Individuals and families expend resources when dealing with a crisis or trauma. In fact, their ability to adapt successfully is dependent on the availability of enough resources to see them through. Those people or families who have sufficient resources and do not have to expend or use up significant resources during times of stress will demonstrate more resiliency and conserve resources for coping with future stresses and traumas (Hobfoll, Johnson, Ennis, & Jackson, 2003; Holahan, Moos, & Bonin, 1997). Resources, as defined in these models, include material goods, vocational/school supports, interpersonal resources, and time and energy.

These theories form the basis for viewing trauma from a family perspective. They help us conceptualize how to intervene with families to empower them to thrive.

## Therapeutic Objectives

Empowering families to recover on their own from trauma is the most fundamental goal of our work. Our Family Adaptation to Trauma Model provides a framework for helping families alter their *Family Stress Reaction* and move from Struggling/Failing to Maintaining/Thriving.

To achieve this goal, it is critical to identify a set of objectives. These objectives suggest where you want to be when you are done. In order to empower families to recover on their own from trauma, we focus on seven objectives. We find that these treatment objectives are valid irrespective of the presenting problem and the cause of the psychological/system trauma.

These objectives are:

1  building rapport and trust;
2  rebuilding safety: eliminating unwanted consequences of trauma;
3  re-establishing structure and regulation;
4  building family social supportiveness;
5  developing new rules and skills of family communication;
6  sharing the family trauma story;
7  building a family healing theory.

Again our Family Adaptation to Trauma Model indicates that empowering families requires adequately considering their *Current Stressor Context*

(Objectives 1 and 2) while strengthening their *Healing Resources* (Objectives 3, 4, and 5) and altering their unhealthy *Perceptions* (Objectives 6 and 7).

## Building Rapport and Trust

Most often the families we see would not seek professional help were it not for exposure to extraordinarily stressful events. Many of these families are extremely uncomfortable seeking help from a professional. They want resolution with a minimal amount of risk and sacrifice. At the same time, they often appear in the initial interview as a group of people who are discouraged, fearful, upset, and suspicious. Our approach is to quickly position the therapist as their respectful advocate who appreciates their pain and is optimistic about their recovery.

A basic ingredient to effective helping is the degree of rapport and trust between the helper and the helpee. This is especially so with families who have experienced trauma. Some therapists have a special gift for establishing rapport and trust very early in the treatment program. Yet, because of the special nature of families impacted by trauma, even the most gifted therapist may be challenged. Therapists are challenged by the family's general sense of mistrust in those who have not experienced the intensity and apparently unique experiences of the traumatic event and subsequent stressors.

Each psychotherapist must utilize his or her own methods. Since the method of treatment that is explicated here is one of empowerment, however, it should be pointed out to the clients that: (1) in most cases the actual therapy will be relatively brief, (2) the role of the therapist is to facilitate positive adaptation and self-reliance, (3) the task of the family is to refine and develop their own skills for coping with extraordinary circumstances, (4) success not only will improve current circumstances but also will enable the family to more successfully cope with future ordeals, and (5) they can individually and as a family be useful to others attempting to cope with similar trauma.

Trust and rapport are also built when the therapist and the family are clear on their respective roles. Consistent with the goal of empowering the family is clarifying the therapist's role, emphasizing at every step of the way that his or her job is to create the right kind of conditions under which the family can find their own way, solve their own problems, and "heal" themselves. The role of the family is easy to define; they are the experts. They know themselves and their particular circumstances. They know their strengths and their struggles.

Over and over we have found that families—be they clients or research participants—are unique. There is a considerable range of functioning—both with or without a traumatizing condition. The therapist's role in helping families deal with trauma is to assess their unique circumstances and enable them to confront these circumstances and thrive by effectively utilizing their current resources and developing the necessary resources to cope more effectively now and in the future.

This is easier said than done, of course. We, psychotherapists, have good intentions, but realizing these intentions is another matter. We are always mindful of the fact that each family has the capabilities to solve any of their problems by themselves with the right kinds of skills, perspectives, guidance, and time. And we have never been disappointed in this regard.

## Rebuilding Safety: Eliminating Unwanted Consequences of Trauma

Rarely do families who have experienced trauma seek treatment without suffering from some unwanted consequences of that experience—be they the classic PTSD symptoms that were noted earlier, unsuccessful efforts to cope, feelings of discouragement, or whatever the family believes is unwanted and linked to the traumatic event. Most often a desire to eliminate these consequences is the major reason why families seek help.

It is highly likely that the experience of trauma has undermined the family's basic sense of safety and efficacy. One of the first tasks of the trauma clinician is to build an understanding of the family's current context and ongoing risk of exposure, and how their fears and uncertainties are impacting their everyday functioning.

We encourage clinicians to quickly acknowledge these consequences and indicate that the primary purpose of any intervention program is to identify and eliminate these difficulties. Our goal in attending immediately and continuously to symptoms and unwanted changes is both to educate the family about trauma and traumatic stress and to reframe these consequences in a way that allows them to go away more easily.

The Murrays, for example, had anticipated that the focus of treatment would be on their daughter and her potential suicide. At the start of their treatment, they needed to focus on making sure their daughter was safe. Once this was accomplished, it became clear that her potential suicide was less a problem and more a symptom of a traumatized system, the goals of treatment shifted, and the father's war experiences and postwar readjustment problems became an added focus. These experiences and problems were reframed from a family perspective as the Murrays explored how the traumas contributed to their collective current concerns.

## Re-Establishing Structure and Regulation

Even in the healthiest of families, traumatic events disrupt everyday functioning and create overwhelming emotional reactions. In some families, restoring daily routines and returning to well-modulated interactions happen quickly and almost automatically. Other families set this as a goal and with some effort are able to return to normal or near normal. Families who come in for treatment are often still struggling with chaos in their daily routines and with interactions that seem to spiral out of control. Alternately, they may have established new routines, taken on new roles, and developed some new interactional habits that worked in the immediate aftermath of the trauma, but are not working any longer.

Empowering these families includes helping them take back control of their daily family life by actively building healthy, effective, and efficient routines that support predictability. It involves helping families set limits and rules that re-establish tolerable standards for expressing emotions and behaviors. Teaching family members new skills for maintaining emotional control while feeling overwhelmed is central to meeting this treatment objective.

## Building Family Supports

If we believe that many families struggle to adapt to trauma and catastrophe as a result of an imbalance between the resources needed to cope effectively and their available resources, helping families find and secure additional resources becomes a logical treatment objective. Social support is one such resource. Social support, or being helpful to another in a variety of ways at the right times, is the most central function of interpersonal and family relationships. Social support is now viewed in the social sciences as one of the most important of human resources (Brownell & Shumaker, 1984; Gottlieb, 1983, 1988; Pilisuk & Parks, 1986; Shumaker & Brownell, 1985).

Research has suggested that those individuals most traumatized by their experiences are the most impaired interpersonally (Figley, 1985b; Green, Wilson, & Lindy, 1985) and that traumatic residue eventually becomes enmeshed in the victim's interpersonal network (Figley, 1983); thus there is a clear need for marriage and family therapy to both improve the support and promote recovery of the network (family) itself (Figley, 1983).

In helping families who have been traumatized, we try to alert family members to the ways in which they effectively support, encourage, advise, and are generally helpful to one another—in contrast to not being helpful—and learn to be even more supportive. This is done through general discussion and in homework exercises that will be discussed later. We extend this focus to social supports that can be sought outside the family, so it is helpful to have families consider their broader network and who else might be able to assist them during stressful times.

Other sources of support also help. We like to consider a broad array of resources that might be available to families when they are in need, including money and financial resources, management of time and effort, and spiritual supports.

## Developing New Rules and Skills of Family Communication

Typically in families unwritten rules emerge over years of interaction that prescribe the manner and content of communication among family members (Watzlawick et al., 1967). Family rituals and secrets stylize and rigidify family interaction, resulting in a pattern of family behaviors that is generally functional in day-to-day activities. However, under traumatic conditions these patterns may be extremely dysfunctional.

A client family struggling with a sudden suspension of the oldest child from school, for example, had great difficulty in clarifying their goals for therapy. Rarely did the family members communicate with each other simultaneously about one issue. Mom was typically the alarm system for family-wide issues (for example, an upcoming holiday or family visit or identifying a problem requiring solution); Dad ensured the three children attended to the issues and declared when the issue was dealt with effectively. Fortunately, Mom attributed the son's new acting-out behavior to a recent auto accident in which the son's best friend had been seriously injured and did not want him to be punished. Dan, the son, did not take the school situation seriously until his mother did so.

We try to make family members aware that the purpose of therapy is to facilitate effective communication about extraordinary events in which the family has very little experience. Family members must become convinced that to do this requires extraordinary methods (rules and communication skills), which they can, if they wish, view as temporary until the problem is solved.

New family rules and communication skills involve those that encourage the free exchange of ideas in a clear and efficient manner. These new rules and skills include both sharing about what happened and listening to others while they tell about it from their own perspective. A portion of the family therapy sessions and subsequent homework should involve teaching these new interaction methods. One of the objectives of this therapy is to create a context for allowing the free expression of emotions and experiences among all family members about anything they view as relevant to their stressful situation. As family members become able to talk about difficult and uncomfortable topics, they develop the skills necessary to share their trauma story.

## Sharing the Family Trauma Story

The objective here is to encourage a retelling of the experiences connected to both the trauma and its emotional wake. Having the entire family listen to the stories of each family member causes new insights to emerge that lead to important alterations in the perception of the situation. Specifically, the family begins to develop a consensus view that can answer the fundamental victim questions: What happened? Why did it happen? How did each family member react initially and subsequently? Will everyone be able to cope if something like this happens again? These perceptions inevitably lead to greater acceptance, as well as understanding, of past and present behavior and attitudes of fellow family members.

An example is the Kelly family (Mary and Don and their children Susan, eleven, and Mike, nine), who sought help in coping with the tragedy of a stillborn baby eight months into pregnancy. Everyone had looked forward to the birth. Disappointed in their efforts to grieve the death of the baby, the family sought the services of a grief counselor six months following the tragedy. The family was shocked to learn that Mike felt some guilt over the death. He felt that he was partly to blame because he felt jealousy and, thus, anger toward the gestating baby for dominating his parents' attention during the pregnancy. He had had numerous nightmares following the miscarriage, but at the time they occurred he could not disclose that the nightmares were associated with his once-felt anger and jealousy. By disclosing these feelings and experiences, he enabled the parents to express their own grief, acceptance of his grief, guilt, and other feelings, and forgiveness of his normal feelings of rivalry toward a sibling. Susan, it was discovered, had denied her feelings and attempted not to think about the trauma in hopes of avoiding the emotional pain and helping her parents recover. It was important to relieve her of such adult responsibilities and give her permission to grieve.

## Building a Family Healing Theory

Many people who have been traumatized work through their experiences by developing new realities about the causes and circumstances of the traumatic event; they build a "healing theory" that fully accounts for what, why, and how it happened and why they acted as they did (Figley, 1979, 1983; Horowitz, 1986). A critical objective in this approach is to help each family member articulate his or her own individual healing theory. Then the therapist can begin to help the family build a family healing theory from the collection of family members' stories and theories. It is critical that the therapist allow the family to struggle with the various views of the trauma and its wake and allow the collective meaning to emerge.

This objective of developing a family healing theory, then, is building a new, more optimistic perspective. It is a set of statements about the circumstances and consequences of the trauma for the family and an optimistic scenario of what would happen if a similar traumatic event took place again. Every family member will *not* embrace this consensus view (family healing theory) with equal enthusiasm. Yet it is essential that every family member recognize the need for such a view and be willing to support it for the common welfare of the family. To achieve this consensus, the family healing theory may need to be rather general and avoid language that is controversial.

## Treatment Techniques

These seven treatment objectives are met using a wide variety of treatment strategies. Some specific techniques are core to the empowering approach we describe. These include:

1  psychoeducation;
2  shared decision-making;
3  family supportiveness relations skills;
4  collaborative coping skills development;
5  co-constructed trauma narrative;
6  making peace with the past.

## Psychoeducation

Families are experts about their past and current situation. They know each other extremely well and often are the best sources of information about how things have changed since the trauma. It is important to access and use all of this expertise, but it is also crucial to equip the family with the necessary knowledge about the traumatic stress recovery process. To accomplish this, we give the parents and older children materials to read. We structure discussions with the family to help explain trauma and traumatic stress to the family. We also talk with the family about the treatment process and the benefits they can expect from taking part. At each step, we explain what we are planning to do and how it will help accomplish the family's goals.

In addition, we believe that it is important to help families develop effective systemic or family resources, such as communication, problem-solving, and conflict resolution skills, to enable them to struggle through what has already happened and to avoid stressful events in the future. Psychoeducational materials are often helpful to families as they learn these new skills.

## Shared Decision-Making

Having equipped the family with the information that they need to understand what is happening to them since the trauma and what treatment options they have, we work with the family to decide on their goals for treatment. As we proceed through treatment, we frequently pause to find out how the family is experiencing treatment, how they would evaluate their progress toward reaching their goals, and whether we are on the right path towards their recovery.

Dr. William Saltzman (personal communication) describes the family goal-setting process:

> Goal setting is a key activity and skill for family-based interventions of all kinds, especially for trauma and grief work. This may best be approached in multiple passes over the course of therapy with initial goals being refined in light of ongoing exploration of family strengths and areas of deficit and increasing knowledge of current and past challenges. The process for developing useful family goals is an active one, with the therapist first guiding a discussion among family members of current concerns and wishes for positive change, then summarizing and gaining family members' assent on prioritization of issues. This task can also be informed by helping family members discriminate between issues or problems that can be addressed in the short term as compared to those that may require a more sustained and concerted effort. Selection of family priorities should involve all family members able to enter into discussion, with developmentally appropriate explanations offered.
>
> Finally, it is important for the therapist to construct goals in positive terms, phrased in terms of increasing a selected behavior or activity rather than diminishing an unwanted behavior, with concrete referents provided of activities or behaviors that would indicate progress toward goal completion. Generally speaking, families should be helped to identify one or two goals to focus on first, and these goals should be crafted such that they have a high likelihood of being achieved.
>
> Once shared family goals are crafted, it can be helpful to track goal status and incremental progress. Each meeting should include a check-in on perceived goal status with a brief exploration of forward and regressive movement. Final sessions can summarize family gains by referencing progress on the selected goals.

## Family Supportiveness Relations Skills

As noted earlier, social support is a critical resource for human survival. This support can take many forms: love, affection, kindness, companionship, a sense of belonging, protection, advice, favors, encouragement. Many other factors often difficult to define and measure are the products of family and friendship relations. There is considerable variation in the quality of social support in all types of systems (for example, work units, clubs, teams). This is certainly the case in families.

Unfortunately, the experience of trauma can interfere with the family social supportiveness. So, we are concerned with building the family's systemic resources, not only to speed their recovery from the current trauma, but also to help them avoid future ones or to recover more quickly if they experience further trauma. This is done by encouraging the family to use social supports and to develop more social support resources within the family as well as within the family's broader network. We strive to assess the degree to which family members are currently supportive to one another, the degree to which they really *want* to be supportive, and the degree to which they are *capable* of being supportive. We offer families a number of concrete ways to evaluate their social support network and to work on increasing social supportiveness.

A major element of treating families, particularly families in crisis, is focusing on the development of a variety of interpersonal relationship skills. These include behaviors that appear to lead to (1) exchanging information between family members effectively and efficiently, (2) communicating openly and directly, (3) deriving pleasure from time spent together, and (4) giving and receiving comfort and nurturance.

By fostering family relations skills, family members are able to fully exploit their own individual resources and those of other family members in helping to seek and resolve the current crisis. There are a wide variety of models for teaching these skills to people within a family context. An excellent example is Guerney's (1977) relationship enhancement (RE) program. Developing interpersonal relationship skills will also be discussed more fully in Chapters five to nine when the treatment approach is discussed.

## Collaborative Coping Skills Development

Some sessions with the family focus on building or strengthening the family's coping skills. These skills include organization, leadership, regulation, resource seeking, joint problem-solving, consensus building, negotiation, and conflict resolution. Specific activities and exercises delivered in developmentally relevant ways can help all family members work together to try out, practice, and master these skills. Techniques used in many trauma treatments to teach stress inoculation to individuals can be tailored for use with families.

## Co-Constructed Trauma Narrative

There is strong empirical support for the inclusion of narrative work in trauma treatment within a family therapy model (Carr, 2000). In individual trauma treatment, the narrative component serves as exposure therapy and also as a means for uncoupling memories of the trauma from uncomfortable physiological responses. As individuals talk about what happened to them, and even detail the worst aspects of their traumatic experience, they can sort through their thoughts and feelings about what happened, clarify and put language to their memories, and, if the therapy environment feels safe, do all of this without becoming triggered and aroused.

## Making Peace with the Past

In these sessions, the therapist attempts to help the family recapitulate the most important factors associated with their trauma and learn to manage the memories of this event more effectively and satisfactorily. The focus is often on understanding and utilizing the family's rituals and routines to mark and move beyond traumatic events. By doing so, they not only effectively cope with the traumatic and posttraumatic stress but also are able to make peace with the past and are better prepared to face current and future challenges.

## Five-Phase Approach to Helping: An Overview

We believe, and the research supports, the use of a staged or phased approach to this empowering, trauma-focused family therapy. The purpose of this phased approach is, first, to help the family eliminate the unwanted consequences of being traumatized. Second, we empower the family to regain control and to learn new skills for dealing effectively with stressors. As the family begins to function as they would have done were it not for these traumatic events, the self-efficacy of the family as a whole and its members in particular is restored. We try to help the families, if necessary, develop new rules and skills of family communication and thereby promote self-disclosure. At this point, the family is ready to talk together about what happened and to develop a "family healing theory" to effectively handle current and future traumatic stressors.

Before detailing our empowering approach, we believe it would be useful to provide a brief overview of how each phase of treatment fits with the others.

**FIGURE 4.1.** The Five-Phase Approach to Helping Families Impacted by Trauma

As you begin to use this approach with your own client families, you may wish to refer to Figure 4.1 as a guide.

As illustrated in Figure 4.1, this five-phase approach first builds commitment (Phase I: Joining the Family) from all members of the family to work toward agreed-on objectives. These objectives, of course, include but are not limited to those set forth in Phase I. Without a minimal degree of commitment from the family, it is unwise to proceed to Phase II, or to any of the later phases. But once the foundation of commitment has been laid we can go on to framing the current presenting problem perceived by the family.

In the second phase (Phase II: Understanding and Framing their Trauma Response), the client family is encouraged to share information about their current context, especially the things in the family's life that are unpleasant and require changing. These things most often include a wide variety of hardships and a description of their family stress reaction, including symptoms associated with a family member's traumatic stress reactions and the breakdown and dysfunction of the family system associated with such distress and disorder.

Once the problems are identified to the satisfaction of all family members who wish to be considered clients, the third phase (Phase III: Building Healing Coping Skills) of the treatment program begins. This phase involves helping the family build or strengthen the relational and coping skills that they will need to adapt successfully to their traumatic circumstances and to deal effectively with future stressors or traumas.

The next building block (Phase IV: Sharing and Healing) is sharing the trauma story and developing a healing theory. This means that the family discover, or are introduced to, ways of thinking about their predicament that are more tolerable and adaptable for family functioning. These new insights or perceptions usually include the basic ingredients for a family healing theory. Like any theory, a family healing theory consists of a set of propositions about a particular situation that is useful in both explaining the current predicament and need for assistance and predicting future outcomes. Through a continuing discussion among family members, such a theory emerges. Though less elegant than most scientific theories, a family's healing theory provides a semantic antidote to or medicine for treating and "curing" the trauma "infecting" the family system.

For the Murray family their healing theory would involve the imposed injustices of postwar emotional adjustment endured by the father, the pressures of dual-career families, and the extraordinary stressors of teenagers, culminating in a display of love and caring within the family system and among family members.

For the Murrays and for most other families, discovering and effectively articulating a healing theory are the climax of a successful treatment program. Yet there is one more very important phase.

The final phase in this treatment program (Phase V: Moving Forward) is bringing the intervention to a successful closure by ensuring that the family clients not only have reached their treatment goals but also are well prepared for future adversities. This phase is either the hardest or the easiest. What is important, however, is getting client families to appreciate their accomplishments of successfully coping with an extraordinary traumatic stressor and to acknowledge that they are sufficiently equipped with the resources (both skills and attitudes/values) necessary for coping with future potential trauma.

## Conclusion

Since the publication of this book in 1989 the approach has become known as "family empowerment therapy" and associated with the assumption that families most often manage traumatic events very well, even in the short run. This chapter attempted to explain the five-phase approach by first tracing its origin from practice-based approaches dating back more than fifty years. The standard model of stress management applies as it does for many other approaches and presenting problems. What is critical in any family therapy strategy or approach is that the family members are engaged and seeking the same outcome: being free of the symptoms that brought them to therapy.

The latter sections of the chapter discussed the family empowerment approach by first discussing its fundamental objectives not only to eliminate unwanted symptoms but to enable the family to do it largely themselves by learning and practicing some basic family communication rules and coping skills that enable members to better appreciate the perspectives of other family members in a safe environment, and building a "healing theory" regarding what happened to this family and its members, how they responded then and now, and what will enable them to move forward with their lives.

Now let us turn to a detailed look at Phase I in the next chapter. Here we will discuss the initial sessions with families who have been traumatized and the process by which we enlist their commitment to the treatment program and its objectives.

# five

# **Phase I**

## Joining the Family

Chapter five considers issues related to "joining" the family, the first step in establishing the necessary trust for trauma work. This kind of family engagement may take several sessions. We first discuss the treatment preconditions for working with the traumatized family client by listing some critical questions that will shape how best to help them. Later we discuss helping families determine whether a family approach to treatment is appropriate for addressing their trauma-related distress.

## Shifting Attention Toward the Family

Working with families impacted by trauma requires shifting the attention of therapy away from either an identified patient/client or victim and toward the family as a whole. This shifting begins as soon as therapy begins. Indeed, the fact that the family is open to considering family therapy and not therapy just for the "victim" is an important distinction that family members should be aware of and be given credit for.

As noted earlier, families are exposed to trauma in many ways (that is, vicariously, indirectly, or directly from inside or outside the system). In most cases the circumstances that led to the family's being traumatized involve only one of its members actually being exposed to a highly stressful event that occurred outside the system. Until recently all or most attention was focused on the victimized member. The family was viewed simply as "next of kin" or, at most, a source of social support that could be useful in the victim's recovery.

Moreover, the family may have sought treatment primarily because of the victimization of one member and agreed to attend therapy sessions as a family in order to help this victim.

Gently but swiftly, the therapist should broaden attention from the victim to everyone in the family. Although the victim may have suffered more emotional harm from the traumatic event, other family members have also suffered, and they require attention and help. The shift of focus can be illustrated in the following statement by a therapist who is seeing a family in which the father had nearly lost his life in a bad automobile accident.

> *Therapist:* I am sure that Dad appreciates your being here to support his recovery from the accident. Yet Dad and I agree that he is not the only "victim" in the family. He is not the only one who has been wounded and frightened and is having difficulty recovering. As we can see from your own stories, everyone in the family has been affected in some way by this terrible ordeal. The family has been the victim of that drunk driver who hit Dad on the way home. So it's our job to help him recover from this accident emotionally, by helping all of you, those he loves, to fully recover and be able to put this nightmarish six months behind you once and for all and move on with your life. Okay?

Sometimes the family member who has been traumatized is more than willing to shift the focus. Occasionally, this is not so. In such a case the therapist may need some time alone with her or him to emphasize the importance of a family-centered approach while at the same time eliciting her or his worries and concerns about shifting attention.

## Treatment Preconditions

As noted in the previous section, shifting attention away from the individual first identified as a victim and toward the family taking responsibility is the essence of empowerment and the right kind of partnership between the therapist and client family. Together they can sort out the important issues, ones most challenging for the family. As we enable the family to take more responsibility to face and fight the disturbing effects of trauma on family life, it is critical to pause. Prior to implementing a treatment plan that includes desensitization or other emotionally charged methods, it is vital to consider if the family is ready to be treated. Also, is a trauma-informed treatment what they or any family member needs?

With some sense of what is involved in our family empowerment approach to treating families who are traumatized, we would like to briefly discuss what we consider to be the important treatment preconditions to designing a treatment program for any particular traumatized family. We hope also to identify the critical elements in any trauma-informed, family-centered treatment approaches. Overall, as practitioners we are constantly thinking about the client family and the best approach to reaching their goals as a family. Here we continue the discussion of engaging the family to gain their trust and help them determine whether a family approach will meet their needs.

All this is an effort toward enabling the family, empowering the family members to take charge of their adversities. This requires courage on the part of the family seeking help with their trauma and commitment to the time and emotional distress required to overcome their trauma-related crisis.

The fundamental requirements to create an optimal therapeutic environment for healing the trauma wounds include first a commitment of time and emotional energy by the family members. For the therapist it is critical that sufficient time is spent on engaging the family: spending sufficient time to connect with each family member, to become a part of their family as a professional helper. In doing so a partnership is struck between the family and their therapist. As the "real issues" emerge and a treatment plan is crafted, the family begin to feel that they are in charge of their treatment program and that they can be active participants in selecting and engaging in family-centered and trauma-informed treatment options and elements.

## Screening for Suitability for Trauma-Informed Family Therapy

It is important to screen families carefully to determine if they are suited for this kind of therapy. The following questions should be answered, if at all possible: (1) What set of circumstances brought this family to treatment? (2) How committed are they as a family? (3) Is systemic psychological trauma a critical issue in this family? (4) How much are family members suffering? (5) Can some method of family relations skills training be developed?

## What Set of Circumstances Brought This Family to Treatment?

Some families seek assistance because they are certain that their difficulties are related to a traumatic event. Others do not link their current difficulties to past traumas. The Murray family is an example of this. They sought assistance out of concern for their daughter. Shortly after gathering background information, however, it quickly became apparent that the family system was struggling to cope with the consequences of past events.

Also, it is important to determine how long the family has endured the traumatic stress. Was it recent, such as the sudden death of a family member? Has it been an ongoing problem that has only now become a crisis?

The circumstances of presenting problems and chronicity are important to planning and beginning the therapy program, since the family must believe that their current difficulties are at least in part linked with traumatic events. This will enable the therapist to proceed quickly once the treatment program begins.

## How Committed Are They as a Family?

Appreciating that the family is struggling with traumatic stress is only one part of the task for the therapist at this point, however. Some families seek professional assistance to have "something fixed" and not to be fixed themselves. For example, parents are more likely to commit to a therapy program that, they are assured, will result in the child's conforming to their wishes than to a program that encourages the parents to change.

Thus, commitment to treatment may be quite high under some circumstances, such as making the youngest child mind his parents. Commitment may be low if the treatment requires the parents to change their parenting methods.

A family therapist treated a family who were court-ordered to seek therapy for their six-year-old son, who had been caught sexually molesting a neighbor's toddler. It was clear that the family only wanted to have the six-year-old treated and that they felt their presence was only to reinforce and "witness" the treatment. It quickly became obvious to the therapist and to the family that the entire family had been traumatized by the event, and they were suffering from shame, anger, and confusion. In a short time the focus of the therapy expanded from the son to his family and eventually to the family of the toddler.

Moreover, clients who have been traumatized not only often deny the long-term negative consequences of the traumatic events but also are often concerned about recapitulating these painful memories. As one forty-year-old father once explained to me: "Doc, how will I know that what I uncover and let out of the bag won't turn on me and I won't be able to get it back into the bag?" If client families understand the treatment process and the ultimate goal of an empowering approach, they are more likely to agree to engage in the hard and often painful work involved and to trust the therapist enough to take on the risks involved.

Families who are traumatized may lack commitment to treatment, then, if it involves dealing with painful memories of the past. It is important in the beginning, however, that therapy not start until and unless clients understand the objectives and course of therapy and are fully committed. At times of uncertainty it is necessary for the therapist and clients to strike a deal that the clients commit to at least a brief trial period of several sessions (say, two to five). At the end of this period the scope and progress of therapy are evaluated.

It is important, irrespective of the means by which it is established, that the entire family be committed to the treatment program. In effect, all members need to be committed and willing to at least *consider* changing their own behavior and relationships with other family members.

## Is Systemic Psychological Trauma a Critical Issue in This Family?

Obviously it is important to establish the fact that we are working with a family impacted by trauma. It is not necessary that *anyone* in the family have a diagnosable case of PTSD to qualify as a "traumatized family." Briefly, the following criteria apply: evidence of at least one highly stressful event experienced by at least one family member and indirectly by at least one other. As we tried to explain in Chapter three, traumatized families are those who are attempting to cope with an extraordinary stressor. This stressor or set of stressors has disrupted their lives, routine, sense of well-being, and confidence in the safety and predictability of daily life.

## How Much Are Family Members Suffering?

In working with traumatized families over the years, we have come to appreciate the fact that some families suffer more than others, even though the families have been exposed to similar stressors and show clear signs of being traumatized. Similarly, I (CRF) have served as a mental health consultant on numerous major catastrophes. Only a small percentage of victims and victimized families avail themselves of professional mental health services, and only a slightly larger percentage actually needs these services. The others are not "suffering" enough. They are able to draw on their own resources and those of their social support networks to carry them through their ordeal.

Even before any assessments are made, an observant therapist should be able to detect clear evidence of hardship. In the best of cases there are general fear, anxiety, and concern about the long-term effects of traumatic events and the prognosis for recovery. In the worst cases, of course, the family is demoralized, helpless, and not working together. Indeed, in many of the worst cases there are physical violence, substance abuse, and other reactions that may be associated with coping with the ordeal.

We have found that it is critical to clearly identify, document, and seek consensus from the family about these unwanted consequences and suffering and make them a part of the objectives of the treatment program.

## Can Some Method of Family Relations Skills Training Be Developed?

This may seem more like an early treatment objective than a precondition. I see it more as the latter because some client families are unwilling or unable to develop such skills. This may be due to one or more members' "not believing in such nonsense."

In treating PTSD in individuals, we make certain that there is some method of stress reduction/relaxation that is utilized by the client. This allows the client to control her or his stress reactions (both in and out of the therapy session), enables the client to gain a sense of mastery and competence over the often feared symptoms of stress reactions, and enables the client to prevent or control the stress reactions associated with future traumatic events or simple stressors.

We believe that helping families recover from trauma requires the utilization (or establishment) of family relations skills, which are isomorphic to the methods of treating individuals suffering from traumatic stress. As noted elsewhere, this includes but is not limited to skills that are linked to social supportiveness: communication skills, empathy, conflict resolution, problem-solving, negotiation, and other observable, measurable behaviors linked empirically to effective family relationships. A case comes to mind of a family who were experiencing a crisis. The father had recently been suspended from the police force of a large city because of his abuse of alcohol. He was receiving treatment for this problem, yet his family was experiencing considerable stress, partly as a result of his substance abuse but mostly because of the pileup of stressors over the previous year or so.

After the first session it became clear that neither the father nor the eldest child (fourteen-year-old son) was willing to develop what they described as "touchy-feely skills" for the sake of the treatment program. Rather, they wanted the therapist to listen to them and come up with some solution that would "fix" the problems they were experiencing.

If the initial assessments establish that some or all family members need at least a minimal level of these skills, a method of skills training needs to be established. Several of these methods of family enrichment or skills training will be discussed in the coming chapters. What is important at this point in the treatment program is to determine the most appropriate program of training if interpersonal skills are indeed lacking.

In the case of the family of the substance-abusing father, they later agreed that improved skills for relating to each other were important to their future as a healthy family. They recognized that, in order for them to take an active role in solving their traumatic stress and preventing and more quickly coping with future events, it was critical that they develop some additional skills.

Briefly, our approach to helping traumatized families emerges from our theoretical orientation to viewing and treating families who are failing to adapt to their traumas, tempered by our genuine respect for the natural resourcefulness of families. We try to empower the family by creating the kind of intervention context that results in the resolution of the traumatizing experience but, just as importantly, that results in the family's giving themselves most of the credit for the accomplishment. Moreover, this approach makes the family feel more confident to face any future traumatic experiences equipped with the necessary information, skills, and problem-solving methods. In subsequent chapters we try to describe in sufficient detail the steps we take in assessing and helping families who have experienced trauma.

## Conclusion

The initial phase of treatment is building with the family a strong commitment to change—to change from their current situation, which is undesirable but safe or at least somewhat predictable, to a new life that is free of traumatic stress. This is done by eliciting and emphasizing the family's major strengths and resources. It also involves identifying the family's attempts to cope, and explaining to the family and enlisting from them support for the treatment objectives. At the same time, it is critical to normalize the existing symptoms, expressing and engendering optimism for a successful treatment program. At the start, it is critical to help the family generate a sense of confidence in the abilities of the therapist to help the client family change and more effectively adapt to their traumatic experiences and memories.

Yet all of us tend to resist change. Our least successful family clients have been those who sought a painless transformation ("You tell us what's wrong and fix it, Doc!"). Our most successful cases, however, have been clients who were fully informed about the course of traumatic stress, recovery, and treatment and were committed to the objectives of the treatment plan. At the least we need a strong commitment to the therapeutic objectives noted above.

Working with families who are traumatized is rewarding because, more than other families who seek professional psychotherapy, they are at a "teachable" or "treatable" moment. They are suffering so much that they are willing to consider some fundamental changes if they are confident that these changes will relieve their traumatic and posttraumatic stress and that they will be able to learn to cope more effectively in the future. Perhaps they will even learn to avoid traumatic events more effectively.

As noted at the start of the chapter, working with families impacted by trauma requires special attention to enabling or empowering the family to take control of their trauma and related adversities. This requires of client families a commitment to change, courage to overcome their various traumatic stress challenges and the troubling memories that provoke the stress, and commitment to the time and energy to overcome their trauma-related crisis.

As noted throughout this chapter, the fundamental requirements to create an optimal therapeutic environment for healing the trauma include joining and engaging with the family and its members, and spending sufficient time to connect with each family member, to become a part of their family as a professional helper. The therapists and the family strike a functional partnership to address the "real issues" through a co-constructed treatment plan to help the family take charge of their treatment program.

## The Murray Family

As a way of illustrating the principles and phases of our approach we will include a brief section at the end of most of the following chapters focusing on the case of the Murray family and their progress through treatment. As noted at the beginning of the book, the Murrays are a fictional family, although their experiences represent those of most of the families we have tried to help over the years.

Tammy's school counselor on the recommendation of a local psychotherapist referred the Murrays to treatment. The family—John, the father, Mary, the mother, Tim, the nine-year-old brother, and even Tammy, the eleven-year-old identified client—were skeptical of the need for *family* therapy. It was Tammy's suicide potential that was the assumed problem and not the family's problem per se.

The task of the therapist was to recognize their confusion and support their reluctance and suggest that we meet for "only a few sessions" in order to get acquainted. During these sessions the therapist was able to successfully build a commitment to the family-centered treatment plan by allowing each family member to tell his or her story and come to recognize that the entire family was struggling with one or more stressors, and that Tammy's problems were simply the most obvious to others and gained the attention of outsiders.

In this case, engagement of the family required both a challenging and a supportive approach. We also need to emphasize that our treatment model depends on successfully empowering the family to step up and do what is necessary for healing and resilience. As with other family-informed treatments, it is critical that families view their working relationship with their therapist as a working partnership of cooperation, commitment, and mutual trust.

# six

# **Phase II**

## Understanding and Framing the Family's Trauma Response

Chapter six covers information gathering, informing, and building commitment to treatment. It provides helpful information for the clinician about how to approach assessment of trauma within the family system and how to deliver the information gathered back to families in a way that educates them about the trauma response and helps them decide how best to cope with the aftermath of their traumatic experience(s). Such an effort is critical both to identifying families who are indeed traumatized and then to designing a treatment program best suited to ensure that they reach their treatment objectives.

Families who have been traumatized, as noted in Chapter three, are sometimes difficult to detect if they do not represent themselves as being traumatized. Some families, of course, recognize the need to work through some particular catastrophe in their life: the death of a family member, some violent victimization, or other circumstances.

Most often, however, families seek help by presenting a problem different than the traumatic event. Through the course of intervention it becomes apparent that the family is traumatized. These families are very difficult to spot, since families who have been traumatized can often function quite well for long periods of time.

The Murray family is an example of a family that appeared to be concerned only with helping their daughter avoid suicidal behavior. However, just under the surface they were struggling with the aftermath of events that began long before the daughter was born.

Conversely, some families endure highly stressful events and show no lasting unwanted effects. It is unwise when helping these families to linger long on such events other than to recognize the family's strength and coping ability. Detecting which family is traumatized and recovering normally and which is recovering poorly is a challenge.

## Assessing the Family's Level of Stress and Trauma Response

In this section, we will discuss the critical components and various methods for assessing family trauma. Helping a traumatized family requires some careful information gathering. This assessment begins by gaining a comprehensive picture of the stressors and traumas impacting the family. It includes a focus on not only each family member's symptoms and perspectives but also the collective, systemic factors that are impacted by trauma. The assessment helps us to build an understanding of the family's adaptation process consistent with the model outlined in Chapter three.

We start the assessment process with a clinical interview. Gathering information about trauma from the family typically occurs over one to three sessions depending on the family's communication style. Following the interview, we often request that family members complete some standard paper-and-pencil instruments that will provide us with additional information about individual, dyadic, or family unit functioning.

We begin with a description of a clinical interview protocol that is helpful for understanding a family's response to trauma. It includes a series of interrelated questions. The answers to these questions provide insight not only into how each family member has reacted to the trauma but also into how the family as a system of interacting and interdependent members has responded.

This series of questions, then, provides the therapist with useful knowledge about the capacity of the client family to cope with highly stressful situations. What is most important in this interview is to determine if the family is traumatized and, if so, what resources they have and to what extent intervention is necessary and sufficient. Some families only need reassurance: someone who can explain to them how traumatic stress evolves and is managed and how the family is progressing normally in that process. They will remember your reassuring comments and your invitation to call or come in anytime to help in the healing process. Other families, rightly or wrongly, will deny that the traumatic event has much of an influence on them. The interview process will allow you to educate them some about trauma and to talk about the possibility that trauma has indeed changed them. The interview helps us understand how the family would answer the five victim questions. Answers to these five questions can represent the degree to which the family impacted by trauma acquire some acceptable degree of understanding about the event and, therefore, are on the way to recovery. Each of the questions will be discussed in turn:

1  **What happened?** "What happened to me or to us?" is a way of saying "Should I worry about this? Should some action be taken now?"
2  **Why did it happen?** By answering this question we hope to determine how to avoid it happening again or the chances that it will happen again.
3  **Why did we act as we did during the event(s)?** This is a question out of concern for one's performance under extraordinary, traumatic circumstances; one is rarely able to view one's self under such conditions.
4  **Why have we acted as we have since the event(s)?** This suggests that one wants to be assured that some symptoms are a direct result of the traumatic event.
5  **What if something like this happens again?** This is, in some ways, a summary of all the others, because people worry about these things, concerned that they may have gotten off lucky this last time, in comparison with the next time, and that it is critical to figure out what to do before that happens.

For those families that acknowledge the role that their traumatic experience is playing in their current problems, the knowledge gained from the clinical interview provides an opportunity for the family and clinician to build a shared understanding of the family's trauma history and response and to reach agreement on the most appropriate and achievable treatment goals. The family trauma assessment interview is simply an opportunity to:

- permit the family to become acquainted with you, the therapist and human being;
- gather qualitative, intuition-driven information on the client family;
- observe family interaction; and
- learn about many characteristics of the whole family system.

Equally important, the therapist is beginning to gain the family's trust by showing genuine compassion, understanding, and acceptance of their ordeal(s), as will be noted later.

## Eliciting the Family's Major Sources of Stress and Trauma

There are a variety of methods for gathering information about a family's trauma history. Including questions about exposure to trauma is part of any good clinical interview with all families. Referring to the model, in this section of the interview we try to elicit a list of stressors ($Sn$), traumatic events ($Tn$), and secondary stressors ($SSn$). This provides us with some indication of the extent to which the family has been burdened by stress.

We start by urging the family to list as many stressors as possible that have been affecting them for the last month, or at least since they began to recognize that there was a problem. We start with a discussion of stressors rather than traumas to assess the family's ability to discuss difficult issues without becoming dysregulated. The interview with the family might go something like the following:

> *Therapist:* I can understand why you would turn to someone like me for your problems. Tell me, in addition to these problems, what other stressors have you had to cope with recently? You know, worries, difficulties, hassles, concerns that require your attention and energy. It doesn't matter to me how large or small; I'd like to make a list of them now. It will help me understand your situation better. Mom, let's start with you.

The task is a rather simple one and allows everyone in the family to participate. We tend to start with the mother because she is often the parent, role model, and spokesperson for the family. By listing the stressors, the family begin to recognize how difficult it would be for any family to cope, irrespective of the circumstances. Moreover, it provides the therapist with a clearer picture of the problems being presented by the family.

We go on to ask about the family's trauma history. We are *not* starting a trauma narrative—we are *not* looking for a detailed description of exposures nor asking the family to process what has happened. We *are* starting to do some gradual exposure by having families list the dangerous and frightening things that have happened to them. The interview might go on with a question something like the following:

> *Therapist:* In addition to stresses and daily hassles, most families also experience some traumatic events over the course of several generations. By traumatic events, I mean experiences that were very scary, dangerous, and potentially life-threatening. Think back about some of the experiences your family has had and tell me about the bad things that have happened to your family.

From many years in working with individual and family clients it became clear that many had experienced more than one single traumatic event. For example, war veterans who had left the military ten to fifteen years earlier had, since the war, experienced a wide variety of catastrophic experiences (for example, auto accidents, tragic losses, and other extraordinary cataclysmic events of living). Moreover, many had been exposed to highly stressful experiences *prior* to military service. That these experiences happened to them was not surprising; and these experiences probably did not occur any more frequently for veterans than for nonveterans.

What is important, however, is that current symptoms of distress and problems in the family may be exclusively associated with one event but may also be associated with many. Therefore, to effectively treat traumatic stress, we need to know the true origin or multiple origins of the stress. We may assume that these symptoms and family concerns are connected only with the most extraordinary catastrophe, such as the experiences of a war, a violent rape, a terrorist attack, or a hostage taking. Yet with some patience we can detect that the family has experienced (and may still be recovering emotionally from) *several* traumatic events.

Finally we ask the family to discuss some of threats to or pressures on the family that are related to their traumatic experiences. We might ask the family a question something like the following:

> *Therapist:* As if the experience of trauma is not hard enough, unfortunately there are often problems or hardships that families have to deal with following exposure to trauma. Sometimes a family has to move if their home has been damaged by a flood or a fire. Sometimes a family has to deal with legal issues related to being the victim of a violent crime. Sometimes a family experiences the loss of or separation from a family member as a result of trauma. These are called secondary stressors and they can add to feelings of distress. Can you tell me about some of the additional concerns or hardships that your family has faced related to the traumas you have experienced? Have you had any losses or separations?

After the stressors are identified, it is important to ask the family to describe how they perceived their stressors and traumas and how they have attempted to cope with each stressor if they have not offered this information already. Again, it is important for everyone in the family to talk. Together these lists (stressors and coping) will form a picture of the family's efforts to manage the posttraumatic period—what has helped and what has hindered recovery.

Finally, we always end this portion of the clinical interview by asking the family to assess their current risk of exposure to trauma. Again, if possible, it is important for each member of the family to share any safety concerns. Obviously, if anyone in the family describes current fears or ongoing traumas, the therapist must be ready to intervene by helping the family develop appropriate safety plans.

Two more formalized methods for talking with families about their stressors and trauma include the traumagram and trauma timeline.

## Traumagram

The traumagram (Figley, 1988b) is somewhat analogous to a genogram since, like a genogram, it guides the therapist to collect specific information that can then be used to chart the traumatic events that have occurred to a family member. Each family member is asked to first identify any traumatic events in her or his life: significant events that were extraordinarily stressful at the time and that left lingering, troubling memories for a time. The rest of the instrument probes for specific dates, the names of those also exposed, and a rating of the degree of stressfulness at the time of the event, twelve months later, and at the time of testing. With these data, then, you are able to construct a traumagram. The traumagram utilizes information about the various distressing events and the period within which the family member strove to cope with the events. Charting the information in this way results in a diagram that shows the various traumatic experiences and resulting stressors endured by family members. Viewed together, the traumagrams of each member of the family provide a family profile of the tracks of trauma. It enables the clinician to view the current struggles in a broader historical context. Traumagrams are very useful to us in tracking individual family members' patterns of stress reactions and coping and viewing, together, the family system's reactions and coping.

## Trauma Timeline

Another method for helping a family develop a picture of their trauma history is to have them develop a trauma timeline. Members of the family make a list of all the traumatic events that they remember. These can include events that happened to the whole family as well as events that happened to any member of the family. The events listed by the family are dated. Approximate dates can be used if the family cannot remember the exact date of the event. For traumatic exposures that were ongoing such as domestic violence or child physical abuse, traumatic events can be listed with a start date and an end date. Between the start and end date, family members may remember particular instances that were worse than others and these traumas can be listed and dated also. Once the family has generated their list, the events can be ordered chronologically, placed on a timeline, or put in the order of least to most stressful (Kiser, 2008).

## Eliciting Signs and Symptoms of Traumatic Distress in Individual Family Members

Next, it is important to talk with the family about the effects of stress and trauma on individual family members. Everyone in the family may be experiencing something different, because there are individual differences in the way people appraise traumatic events, cope with their thoughts and feelings about what happened, and express any discomfort they are having. Developmental stage and gender also influence the way that people react to trauma. As you talk with the family to assess the level of traumatic distress that individual members are experiencing you will also be helping the family to understand how varied their responses are even when they might all have been exposed to the same event. Positive family adaptation to trauma means that the family is able to successfully negotiate the traumatic stress reactions of all of their members.

We usually start by talking to the family about common reactions to stress and trauma. We provide them with information about the clinical disorders and symptoms that are typically associated with trauma. We then ask them to share with each other any problems or concerns they have been experiencing or to gently talk about what they have observed in each other.

## Understanding the Relationship Between Traumatic Stress and Family Functioning

Finally, our interview focuses on the impact of trauma on the family and how it functions. Both short- and long-term changes have been noted in research and clinical practice. Particularly vulnerable are family structure, relations, and coping (Kiser & Black, 2005). We discuss each along with suggested questions for exploring important dimensions with the family. We also provide some examples of tasks that the family can be asked to do during the interview. These tasks provide an excellent opportunity for the therapist to observe family interaction and functioning.

Again, using the Family Adaptation to Trauma Model, the clinical interview helps elicit information about *Family Stress Reaction* which is critical to developing a plan for healing. As the clinician asks the family about their structure, relations, and coping, a picture of the family's adaptation to trauma emerges—how does the family view the stressors and traumas they face (*Family Perceptions*) and are the resources available and used by the family to deal with stress and trauma (*Family Healing Resources*)? This information supports our empowerment approach, which emphasizes fully developing the family's natural resources such as family management, social supportiveness, and family relations skills.

# Structure

## *What Happens Every Day in This Family?*

Has this family's routine changed since the trauma? Families usually organize their day with simple routines and sometimes more elaborate rituals. These routines and rituals help families accomplish the tasks of daily living and regulate daily interactions. These are often disrupted by a traumatic experience and families are challenged to find ways to re-establish their daily structure as soon as possible. If the traumatic exposure is accompanied by significant loss and many secondary stressors, returning to a daily routine can be delayed. Asking the family to tell about a typical day in their home will provide lots of interesting information about the family's organization and will also allow the clinician to observe family communication.

## *How Flexible Are Family Roles?*

Families today have much more flexible family roles than did earlier generations. This is partly because more women work outside the home, forcing husbands and children to do more at home today than in the past. But there tends to be a wide variation among today's families regarding who performs what family role beyond simply cooking, cleaning, and repairing things. This includes such roles as shopping for the family's food, clothes, household appliances, and furniture; communicating for the family; protecting the family against intruders, fire, or bad weather; and so on. What is critical in families experiencing a crisis is not who performs these tasks but the extent to which they are shared among at least two family members. It is critical because these families may have members who are unable, from time to time, to perform their duties. Hardy or effective families are able to rely on another family member to perform these vital family functions.

## *How Do Adults in the Family Provide Leadership and Support for the Children?*

It is important to understand the role of adult caregivers in the family, how they work together to raise the children, and how they feel about their parenting role. Trauma can have a significant impact on the ability of adults in the family to fulfill leadership and parenting responsibilities.

## *Does the Family Structure Provide Family Members With a Sense of Safety?*

Families use routines and limits to establish predictability and consistency. They put into practice strategies for monitoring the comings and goings of family members and for staying in touch with each other when not together. Talking with the family about how this worked before the trauma and also about changes since the trauma occurred help them consider their present and future safety needs. Talking directly with families about how routines can support safety is encouraged.

## Relational Factors

Cohesion, communication, and cooperation are extremely important relational factors in understanding and helping families who have experienced trauma.

### How Cohesive Is This Family as a Group?

Do family members like to be with each other as much as they would if they were not in the same family? This is an interesting question to ask yourself when you first meet a family. It gives you a sense of how well they work and cooperate with one another. Functional, hardy, effective families tend to enjoy each other's company, though they may wish not to be together all the time when they have an opportunity. This is particularly true for teens. Has the traumatic experience changed the way family members spend time together? Are family members closer or more distant?

### What Are the General Levels of Tolerance for One Another in This Family?

Is the family more or less tolerant in times of crisis? Families who cope best become more tolerant and tend to overlook minor violations of social or family rules. Families who cope poorly with stress tend to be even less tolerant than usual in stressful situations, particularly crisis situations. It is as if they adopt a philosophy of "every man for himself" during these times, during which there are few indications that family members look out for each other's welfare.

### How Committed Are Family Members to One Another?

Similarly, we try to detect the extent to which family members are committed to one another: for protection, emotional comfort, and companionship. In times of stress or trauma, does the family rally around each other, provide support and protection for vulnerable members, and believe that what is good/bad for one member of the family is good/bad for the whole family?

### How Much Affection Is There in This Family?

Relatedly, hardy families appear, in both words and actions, to be genuinely affectionate toward one another. Some families rarely demonstrate this affection; there is an absence of kissing, hugging, and even touching. Yet the affection among members is demonstrated by frequent smiles, friendly banter, and general attentiveness. This is in contrast with troubled families, who appear ill at ease not only with the therapist but also with each other.

*What Are the Quality and Quantity of Communications
Among Members in This Family?*

For the family dealing with trauma, good communication among family
members is critical to recovery (see, for example, Figley, 1983, 1985c). A family
that fits the following description tends to have reasonably good quality and
quantity of family communications: Anyone may talk about anything at any
time as long as it is done with at least a minimum amount of courtesy.
Moreover, it appears that messages sent are received and acknowledged as they
were meant. There is little serious quibbling over semantics. Adequate display
of and commitment to understanding and empathy toward one another are
apparent. These signs, of course, are just that—brief indicators. Hundreds of
books are filled with discussions about interpersonal and family communication. Moreover, more than a dozen measures are available that purport to
quantify these factors. But careful observation of the family during sessions will
reveal an enormous amount of information.

*Do Family Members Tend to Utilize or Avoid Resources
Outside the Family?*

It is rather odd that families that most need outside resources such as family
therapy are often the most resistant in seeking them. We find that knowing
about the family's history of resource utilization is helpful in planning
treatment. For example, various support groups, continuing education classes,
skills training, and other supplemental interventions would be very useful in
augmenting therapy for families who have been traumatized.

*Do Family Members Serve as a Resource to Others as Well?*

We have found that families who frequently provide resources to others, such
as donations to charities, performing services through places of worship or
service clubs (for example, Lions Club or Girl Scouts), or various acts of
kindness such as donating a meal to a grieving family, tend to be families who
are more open to help from others. Giving and an altruistic spirit are often
related to recovery from catastrophic events.

## Coping

Recall that back in Chapter three the typical coping characteristics that distin-
guish between functional and dysfunctional family coping were identified. We
have found that it is useful to identify the characteristic ways client families
cope with catastrophic events. Following are some questions that address each
of the major family coping characteristics. The information such questions
produce will be useful in developing the specific ways in which we try to help
the family.

## *Do Family Members Have a Clear Understanding and Acceptance of the Sources of Stress Affecting Them?*

Families impacted by trauma are easier to help if they can identify the cause–effect or stressor–stress reaction paradigms that apply to their circumstances. In contrast, client families who are confused about how or why they are dysfunctional or who have major differences among family members in beliefs or perceptions—particularly between parents and children or husbands and wives—present more challenges. Some families simply have had no opportunity to focus on their circumstances and may thus require some time and discussion to adequately address this question.

## *Do Family Members See the Difficulties They Face to Be Family Centered, or Do They Blame One or Two Family Members?*

It is often simple to predict in the initial interview which client family will cope well with adversity and will require only a few therapy sessions. These are families who will move (or have already moved) quickly from blaming or finding fault with a family member to recognition that everyone in the family shares both the blame and the credit for their current predicament. This is particularly true for the parents' assumption of responsibility. Families who are likely to adapt positively recognize (1) that irrespective of what caused the problems they face the family faces them together, (2) that the entire family is being affected by this crisis, and (3) that it will require everyone's cooperation to solve the problem. Indeed, many of these families tend to be better off as a result of their struggles, which we will discuss later. Assignment of a task to pick and discuss a mildly stressful event that occurred in the family can be a valuable way to observe how family members make attributions.

## *Do Family Members Appear to Be Solution Oriented or Blame Oriented?*

Similarly, we have found that there is a good prognosis for families who tend toward actively solving a problem and whose members avoid blaming each other. This does not mean that these families do not spend sufficient time tracking the causes of their difficulties. It is unwise to move too quickly to solve a problem when there is uncertainty about exactly what constitutes the problem. However, members of families who tend to maintain long-felt resentments, lack trust in one another, and feel discouraged in life tend to blame other family members for past and present circumstances. These families will require considerable attention and patience in working through their traumatic experiences and shifting their patterns of family relationships to more supportive and protective ones. We believe that including a brief problem-solving task during the clinical interview is ideal for observing the family's ability to use collaborative skills in generating solutions.

*Do Family Members Share Religious or Spiritual Beliefs
That Help Guide Their Perceptions and Understanding
of What Happens to Them?*

Have the family's beliefs helped them explain why trauma has happened to their family? Have their religious practices and community been a support during difficult times? Hardy or resilient families often lean on strong spiritual beliefs and religious practices to help them cope when bad things happen. Traumatic experiences can also threaten these strongly held beliefs and interrupt the practice of religious rituals and routines.

*Is There Evidence of Family Violence?*

Sometimes families impacted by trauma, overwhelmed with emotion and stress, resort to displays of aggressive behavior. For some families, physical violence may have emerged as a coping method, albeit a poor one, to solve problems or at least manage unwanted behavior. The use of physical violence may be an isolated incident or may be a part of the pattern of behavior between a parent and children, between husband and wife, or among siblings. Rarely are families satisfied with such patterns, but they tend to become stuck with them. We have found that it is very important to specifically ask about the use of violence. Are there any household rules about physical contact and aggression? What are the consequences if violence does occur? If there is evidence of violence in the family, it is necessary to quickly seek and secure a commitment to substitute other methods for these abusive ones.

Moreover, as soon as possible, the therapist needs to meet with the victim or victims of such aggression and do this without calling attention to the abuse in order not to put the victim at greater risk. In the interview the therapist makes certain that the victim(s) is/are not in any danger and determines if the abuse has been or should be reported and if it is wise to proceed with this treatment program at this time.

Sometimes it is clear that the abuse is much more important to the family than the "presenting" trauma. Irrespective of which trauma is the initial focus, we always attempt to address all traumatic stressors generally in the order that the family can deal with them. Most often this means easiest and most recent first, assuming that the family's skill and knowledge about coping are cumulative.

*Is There Evidence of Substance Abuse in the Family?*

Similarly, various forms of substance use and abuse may be part of the family's difficulties and may have started as a method of coping long before the traumatic event. We have found that any addiction problems will become especially evident during the family's efforts to recover from traumatic stress. Sometimes it may be necessary to address the addiction problem in combination with treating the trauma. It is important to evaluate the role of substance use and abuse in the family and to help individual family members address these concerns as part of the family healing process.

## Standardized Measures of Family Trauma

In addition to the clinical interview, a good assessment will include psycho-metric measures of the family's traumatic stress and the resources available to cope with these stressors. A comprehensive assessment of each family member, family subsystem, and the family as a whole is a daunting task for the clinician, but especially for the family. Thus it is important to carefully choose the issues and concerns where the information obtained from standardized measures is necessary for case conceptualization and treatment planning and monitoring. Use of standardized measures to augment the clinical interview is critical not only in planning the treatment program but also in evaluating whether the treatment is working once the program is implemented.

There are many reliable and valid instruments used to assess exposure, traumatic response, general functioning, and coping in children, adolescents, and adults. Likewise there are multiple choices when looking for measures of marital, parenting, and family functioning and coping. Table 6.1 provides information on some psychometrically sound and widely used instruments (adapted from Collins et al., 2010).

## How and When to Administer Assessments

If a traumatic event was linked to the family's problems prior to the first interview, the family should be asked to complete these instruments along with the standard intake forms administered to most of your clients. Doing this will allow you to prepare more completely for the clinical interview and to form some preliminary hypotheses about the family dynamics associated with the present problems.

If you discover that trauma is an issue for the family during the course of treatment, you should administer the selected instruments to each member of the family as soon as possible after you suspect that you are dealing with a traumatized system. The assessments can—and most often *should*—be com-pleted between sessions without collaboration among family members. It is advisable to limit the entire battery so that family members spend no more than an hour to an hour and a half on completing them.

The results are quite useful in building the treatment program by tailoring it precisely to the problems, strengths, and needs of each family. Partly as an incentive for completing the tests and partly as an educational tool, we inform

**TABLE 6.1. Family Trauma Assessment Instruments**

| | Construct | Instrument | Description | Age | Administration |
|---|---|---|---|---|---|
| Adult | Exposure | Life Events Checklist | Screens for exposure to potentially traumatic events during a respondent's lifetime. | Adult | Respondents indicate type of exposure (personal experience, witnessing, etc.) to 16 different events. Developed to be administered with the Clinician Administered PTSD Scale (CAPS) but can be used separately. |
| | | Childhood Trauma Questionnaire (CTQ) (Bernstein & Fink, 1998) | Caregiver history of abuse/neglect during childhood. The scale assesses three types of abuse (emotional, physical, sexual), two types of neglect (emotional, physical), plus two validity scales. | 12+ | Twenty-eight-item self-report measure which takes about five minutes to complete. |
| | Distress and functioning | PTSD Checklist (PCL) (Weathers et al., 1993) | Assesses DSM-IV diagnostic criteria for PTSD. | Adult | Seventeen items that take about five minutes to complete. May be scored dichotomously (presence or absence of PTSD) or continuously (to measure symptom severity). The respondent is asked to rate how much the problem described in each statement has bothered him or her over the past month. |
| | | Clinician Administered PTSD Scale (CAPS) (Blake et al., 1995) | Structured diagnostic interview to assess DSM-IV diagnostic criteria for PTSD. | Adult | Thirty items which take about one hour to review with the client. |

| | | Measure | Age | Description |
| --- | --- | --- | --- | --- |
| | | Brief Symptom Index (Derogatis, 1993; Derogatis & Spencer, 1982) | Adult | Inventory of psychological symptoms. The BSI yields three global indices of distress, Global Severity Index (GSI), and nine subscales including anxiety, depression, hostility, obsessive-compulsive, somatization, interpersonal sensitivity, phobic anxiety, paranoid ideation, psychoticism. Self-report measure includes fifty-three items which take about ten to fifteen minutes to complete. |
| Child | Exposure | Traumatic Events Screening Inventory for Children-Brief Form (TESI-C-Brief) and Parent Report (TESI-PR) (Ghosh-Ippen et al., 2002; Ribbe, 1996) | 3–18 years | A measure of experiencing and witnessing of traumatic events for children. TESI-C-Brief covers sixteen categories of events arranged hierarchically. Interview format or as self-report; parent report available. Usually takes twenty to thirty minutes to administer but can take longer depending on the number of exposures endorsed. *A parent-report version for young children (0–6 years) includes traumas more frequently occurring to young children (i.e., animal attacks, prolonged or sudden separations, and intense family conflict).* |
| | Distress and functioning | Clinician Administered PTSD Scale for Children (CAPS-CA) (Nader, Kriegler, Blake, & Pynoos, 1994) | 8–15 years | A measure of DSM-IV diagnostic criteria for PTSD. The measure determines exposure to events meeting DSM-IV criterion, frequency and intensity for the seventeen symptoms in criteria B, C, and D, and criterion E, the one-month duration requirement. Semi-structured interview which includes thirty-five items and takes approximately forty-five minutes to complete. CAPS-CA includes iconic representations of the behaviorally anchored five-point frequency and intensity rating scales, opportunities to practice with the format before questions, and a standard procedure for identification of the critical one-month period for current symptoms. |

**TABLE 6.1.** Continued

| Construct | Instrument | Description | Age | Administration |
|---|---|---|---|---|
| | UCLA PTSD Reaction Index (Pynoos, Rodriguez, Steinberg, Stuber, & Frederick, 1998) | Instrument keyed to DSM-IV PTSD symptoms for youth who report traumatic stress experiences. | 7–12 years | Twenty-two symptom-related items which take about fifteen to twenty minutes to review using an interview format. Parent-report version is also available. An overall PTSD severity score is calculated by summing the scores for each question that corresponds to a DSM-IV symptom and a PTSD severity subscore is calculated for criterion B, C, and D symptoms. A score of 2 on each of the seventeen questions is considered as the symptom cutoff score for each question, and a score greater than 22 is considered the cutoff for moderate PTSD. |
| | Trauma Symptom Checklist for Children (TSCC) (Briere, 1996) | A measure of PTSD and related symptoms, including those related to complex trauma disorders (Roth, Newman, Pelcovitz, Kolk, & Mandel, 1997). TSCC comprises two validity scales and six clinical subscales (anxiety, depression, anger, posttraumatic stress, sexual concerns, dissociation). | 8–16 years | Self-report measure that includes fifty-four items (Version A-forty-four items); no reference to sexual concerns). Can be completed in about twenty minutes. *A parent-report version is available for younger children (TSCYC).* |
| | Child Behavior Checklist | | 6–18 | Requires a parent to rate, on a three-point |

| | | | |
|---|---|---|---|
| | (CBCL) (Achenbach & Edelbrock, 1991) | years | scale, each of 118 problems as they are perceived to reflect the child's behavior over the past six months. The clinical cutoff score for the CBCL is a T-score of 63 or greater, with 60–63 considered in the borderline range of psychopathology. Youth and teacher report also available. A *version for young children (1.5–5 years) is also available.* |
| Family | Couples adjustment | | |
| | Dyadic Adjustment Scale (Spanier, 1976) | Adult | Measure of intimate partner relationships applicable to both unmarried and married couples. It assesses four areas: dyadic consensus, dyadic satisfaction, dyadic cohesion, and affectional expression. | Self-report measure includes thirty-two items and takes five to ten minutes to complete. Shorter versions are also available, including a fourteen-item Revised Dyadic Adjustment Scale (RDAS) (Busby, Crane, Larson, & Christensen, 1995), which retains three of the original subscales and a seven-item Abbreviated Dyadic Adjustment Scale (ADAS or DAS-7) (Hunsley, Best, Lefebvre, & Vito, 2001; Sharpley & Cross, 1982), which includes a single factor. |
| | Conflict Tactics Scales (Straus, Hamby, Boney-McCoy, & Sugarman, 1996) | Adult | Scales measuring the physical and psychological attacks on a partner in a marital, cohabiting, or dating relationship. Also looks at use of reasoning or negotiation to deal with conflicts. Scales | Seventy-eight items that take ten to fifteen minutes to complete. Respondents rate their and their partner's behavior on an eight-point scale. Half of the items relate to the respondent's behavior, and half relate to the partner's behavior. A short form is also available. Also, the CTS2-CA |

**TABLE 6.1. Continued**

| Construct | Instrument | Description | Age | Administration |
|---|---|---|---|---|
| | | | | is an adolescent-report version of the Conflict Tactics Scales. Used as a child report of the parents' behavior towards one another. |
| Parenting | The Parenting Stress Index (PSI) (Abidin, 1990) | Parental distress (contributing parental factors), difficult child (contributing child factors), parent–child dysfunction interaction. | Adult | Self-report measure for parents of children 1 month to 12 years. Full PSI is 120 items; short form consists of thirty-six items. Full PSI takes twenty to thirty minutes; short form estimated to take less than ten minutes. |
| | Parenting Sense of Competence Scale (Gibaud-Wallston & Wandersman, 1978) | Measure covers two factors: parent satisfaction and parental self-efficacy. | Adult | Each item is scored on a six-point Likert scale from strongly disagree to strongly agree. Older version was written for parents of infants; more recent version was written for parents of older children. Seventeen-item self-report that can be completed in less than ten minutes. |
| Family unit | Family Assessment Device (Epstein, Baldwin, & Bishop, 1983) | Designed to measure family functioning based upon the McMaster model. The instrument provides scores for seven scales, including problem-solving, communication, roles, affective responsiveness, | 12+ | Sixty items which take about fifteen minutes to complete. Items are scored on a four-point scale from 1, "Strongly disagree," to 4, "Strongly agree." Clinical cutoff scores indicating healthy versus unhealthy functioning have been established with sensitivity and specificity. A twelve-item version measures general |

| Measure | Description | Age | Administration |
|---|---|---|---|
| | affective involvement, behavior control, and overall functioning. | | functioning. |
| Family Adaptability and Cohesion Scale (FACES IV) (Olson, Gorall, & Tiesel, 2007) | Based on the circumplex model. Revised version includes six subscales: two assess the mid-ranges of adaptability and cohesion, and four assess the extremes (rigid, chaotic, disengaged, and enmeshed). | 12+ | Self-administered instrument each family member can complete. Forty-two items (plus ten-item Family Communication Scale and ten-item Family Satisfaction Scale). |
| Family Assessment of Needs and Strengths-Trauma Exposure and Adaptation (FANS-TEA) (Kiser et al., 2009) | The FANS-TEA assesses the family's exposure to a variety of traumas and contextual stressors and provides a rating of needs and strengths for individual family members (both adults and children), adult intimate partnerships, intergenerational relations, caregiving and parent–child relationships, and sibling relations. | All ages | Completed by the clinician following a one- to three-session interview with the family. |

Adapted from Collins et al. (2010); Family Informed Trauma Treatment (FITT) Center (2010).

our families that they will receive a report in a few weeks and that the results will be explained to them.

We have found over the years that administering the instruments (other than the clinical interview) again every eight to ten sessions and six months after treatment yields valuable benchmarks for tracking progress and recovery. If there is any need for crisis intervention or future therapy sessions, the data will be invaluable to you or any other therapist.

## Framing the Family's Response to Trauma

Once we have completed the assessment, we are ready to build momentum for the next step in this phase of the treatment program. We use the assessment results to guide our understanding of the family's trauma experience and use this understanding to help guide the family toward making an informed choice about how to heal. We use the following seven guidelines to accomplish this step:

## Guideline 1: Conceptualizing the Family's Trauma Response

Administering the clinical interview and a well-designed battery of standardized paper-and-pencil measures to our clients provides extremely valuable information. Among other things, these assessments tell us about how the family members are functioning under what conditions and the elements that would be most useful in a treatment program. Equally important, the assessments tell us about the family system's stressors, perceptions, resources, family stress reactions, and prognosis for maintaining/thriving. We review all of the information shared by the family to formulate our own answers to the five victim questions, as noted earlier in this chapter:

1  What happened?
2  Why did it happen?
3  Why did this family act as they did during the event(s)?
4  Why have they acted as they have since the event(s)?
5  What if something like this happens again?

This clinical case formulation becomes the foundation for working with the family to develop a targeted treatment plan.

## Guideline 2: Viewing the Family as the Expert

Once we have a coherent picture of the family's trauma response, we want to make sure that the family share this understanding and are full partners in their treatment. After all, the family is the ultimate expert on their own experience, reactions, needs, and preferences.

We suggest a partnering approach that encourages information sharing and co-learning through respecting and blending the complementary expertise of the family and their therapist. For a successful therapeutic relationship to develop, the clinician–family partnership must agree on a common language for labeling events and consequences, effective and direct communication strategies, and a shared and informed decision-making process regarding treatment.

We encourage the use of a shared decision-making process in which the family and the therapist share relevant information to enable family-centered selection of treatment alternatives. To facilitate this process, families need to have enough information to make informed choices, and this information needs to be shared with them in a manner that respects their ability to decide on a course of action that best meets their needs and preferences. What is essential in this empowerment process is enabling families to accurately see where they are on the Family Trauma Adaptation thermometer (Thriving? Maintaining? Or are they Struggling or even Failing?) and to determine where they want to be.

## Guideline 3: Normalizing Reaction to Traumatic/Posttraumatic Stress

Many families who seek help in recovering from a traumatic event are bewildered, confused, and discouraged. Members are uncertain if they will ever be able to fully recover from their predicament. It is reassuring when an expert at helping families cope with trauma normalizes their situation and notes that their reactions are common and predictable. Indeed, a quite effective method is the use of "positioning" (Fraser, 1989): taking a position that is directly in contrast to that of most of the family's friends and other supporters. Most often, these people feel sorry for the family's traumatic experiences and urge them, one way or another, at some time or other, to "put the past behind you, forget it, and move on." A therapist might say the following:

> *Therapist:* I can understand the advice of many of your kin in their hoping that not thinking about the event would make it go away. Sometimes that works with more minor events, doesn't it? But based on what you shared

with me during the assessment, I don't think that strategy will work, do you?

Most families who have endured a traumatic event or period in their lives hope that they can begin to put their lives back together as soon as possible and believe that this can be done by simply forgetting about what has happened and moving on. This strategy sounds reasonable, since the past cannot be undone and dwelling on it further appears to be useless and often upsetting. Yet forgetting it is rarely effective unless accompanied by a genuine belief that family members are now safe from harm and prepared to cope with any future traumatic events. Many families are able to gain this perspective and preparedness and move on unimpaired by the traumatic memories. Yet those who cannot will continue to display the characteristic symptoms of traumatic stress—both as individual family members and as a system.

The therapist goes on here to review the problems and issues that the family shared during the assessment. The therapist gives them facts and information about how other individuals and families have reacted in similar circumstances. If individual family members meet the criteria for psychiatric disorders, the therapist labels these and talks about common symptoms.

*Therapist continues:* You know that many of the reactions, feelings, and changes in yourselves and your family are quite common. Other families who have experienced what you have describe similar issues. But frankly I am quite impressed with how well you have done in spite of your ordeal, especially in addition to all the other stressors you listed earlier. I am quite impressed that you have come through all of this as well as you have. Don't be too discouraged when your situation gets worse rather than better in the coming weeks. It's perfectly normal. As a matter of fact, it suggests that your recovery process has really begun.

There is a suggestion of regression in the recovery process. This statement provides both reassurance and normalization of the symptoms because often the process of recovery from a traumatic event includes this pattern. More importantly, however, it sets the family up not only to expect these patterns but also to view them as a sign of progress.

## Guideline 4: Promoting Understanding and Acceptance

The fourth guideline we follow in helping families attempt to conceptualize or frame their trauma-related problems or challenges is promoting empathy among family members, an understanding and acceptance of others. Like the previous guideline, this one also promotes basic family or interpersonal skills. Specifically, promoting understanding and acceptance of fellow family members is not the same as *agreeing* with them. As one family member said, "You mean we should try to understand and accept another's views as their own, but don't have to say it makes any sense or agree with it ourselves?"

The family is attempting to recover from a highly stressful event that has shaken the stability—and in some cases the very existence—of the family. Family members need to be encouraged to accept the need to hear the views of everyone so that they can both account for why they acted as they did and are acting now and, more importantly, accept these past actions. Obviously, future actions may not be so tolerated.

By establishing this and related guidelines in the family, at least insisting on it during therapy sessions, the family can more easily work as a team, work collectively to share individual perspectives about their common family problems. This will greatly facilitate efforts to reach a consensus about the adversities faced by family members perceived or framed in a way that will promote effective actions for coping with the adversities now and in the future.

## Guideline 5: Building Commitment to the Treatment Process

As we tried to demonstrate in the initial chapters of this book, families who have been traumatized often struggle with a large and sudden set of highly stressful situations. They attempt to cope as best they can and for one or more reasons seek professional help. For many families this is the very first time they have sought any kind of professional mental health services—either as a family or as individual family members. Therefore, the effort to contact and face an expert on family relations, as well as a psychotherapist, can be extremely upsetting for some or all of the family members.

Commitment and trust are critical elements in psychotherapy treatment methods. The early phase of any systematic, professional intervention is primarily dedicated to building a sound therapeutic alliance between therapist and family clients. Without it, clients are not only reluctant to change but also unwilling to take necessary risks. They need to be convinced that it will be worth the effort.

Trust and rapport with families impacted by trauma are especially important. Even when families finally decide to seek professional help, they may still be quite reluctant to talk about their traumatic experiences. Irrespective of their presenting problems with the trauma, they will probably be unwilling to disclose all of the details of the troubling events and the subsequent traumatic stress reactions unless they are assured that you know what you are doing, care about them, and want to help. It is important, especially in the beginning, to convey respect for all family members and an appreciation for their suffering. It is also essential to convey a sense of confidence, authority, and experience as a therapist who has dealt with other, equally difficult cases. Simultaneously, their goals for treatment and commitment to the treatment program will emerge.

## Guideline 6: Explaining and Enlisting Support for Specific Treatment Objectives

As the problems, stressors, and attempts at coping are explained by the clients, it is important to begin to translate them into some reachable clinical goals. Although these goals or objectives may change, or others may be added later, it is important to establish a clear working arrangement with the clients about what they hope will happen as a result of the treatment program. Moreover, both the clients and the therapist will have a much better idea of what changed *when they are finished*. Following is an example of what the therapist might say in clarifying the current objectives expressed or implied by the clients:

> *Therapist:* So it sounds like it has been a real struggle for all of you, that you want to rid yourselves of as many of these stressors as possible, get your lives back in order, and have some confidence that if anything as catastrophic as this happens again you'll be ready. Right? As you were describing all your many sources of stress and all the ways you've tried to cope with them and thinking about why you came to me in the first place, I think we came up with a reasonable list of goals for us to reach during our time together. Shall I read them to you? Then let's take them one at a time and see what you think.

## Guideline 7: Expressing Optimism for a Positive Treatment Outcome

Another method of building commitment to the therapeutic objectives is placing these objectives and their connected problems, stressors, and coping efforts and resources into a more positive perspective. Family members are often quite relieved to hear an expert indicate not only that what they are experiencing is normal but also that one can recover fully from these symptoms. It is helpful for the therapist to provide some evidence of the effectiveness of trauma treatment. The therapist can share his or her own successes and also talk about the solid research findings that suggest that trauma treatment works.

However, we have found that such optimism must be calibrated and timed to fit the situation. Too much optimism too early may trivialize and minimize the family's ordeal; too little too late may have no impact at all. It should be viewed as seasoning for a dinner of therapy.

There are at least three ways of building optimism. These are reframing, comparing, and splitting. We will discuss each briefly:

- **Reframing.** Family therapists often discuss the use of "reframing," or attaching a different frame or perspective to the problem. Indeed, an example is the use of "challenge" rather than "problem." This clearly relates to the systemic adaptation-to-trauma process model described earlier. The most critical factors are the perceptions both prior to and especially following the traumatic event. But simply applying new meanings to heretofore traumatic experiences is easier said than done. Such meanings emerge gradually but can be greatly facilitated with our help.
- **Comparing.** Another method of expressing or generating optimism for a positive treatment outcome and, by doing so, building commitment to the therapeutic objectives is the method of comparing. This is discussing one or more other client families who successfully recovered from a similar (or worse) traumatic event. If applicable, the therapist can briefly discuss her or his own experience with a traumatic event and the rocky road and eventual road to recovery or the success she or he has had with families in similar predicaments. We have learned to be careful with this method, however. If comparisons are not presented carefully, some families or at least some family members may get the idea that you do not appreciate the degree of distress and pain caused by their trauma, that theirs is not unique and thus not a cause for alarm. An example of what has worked in the past would be:

  *Therapist:* I can see that this [traumatic experience] has taken a major toll on your family and each of you in differing ways. Had I not worked with other families in similar situations, I guess I would not feel as hopeful right now. But I have. It's like a prizefighter who is down for the last count, "eight," "nine"—and goes on to win the fight. It feels just horrible now, but you're not out yet. I can tell you have what it takes to overcome these terrible adversities.

- **Splitting.** This final method is clearly the most difficult to use yet may be the most powerful with some families in generating hope for treatment. This method involves "splitting" with another expert's less optimistic opinion about the prognosis of the family. This enables the therapist to "voice" the family's worst fears through the opinions of an expert—a colleague, textbook, or media report about families confronted with the same set of challenges (for example, "trauma tends to destroy families"). At the same time the therapist can take issue with (or "split" from) this position because of the unusual strengths and characteristics of the client family.

It is impossible to say which approach will work best for which family. Moreover, one approach may work best with some members, another approach with other members of the same family.

## Summary and Conclusion

Our task in this second phase, then, is to encourage the client family to frame the problem. We are looking here for the building blocks for a healing theory, a statement of what, how, and why this terrible thing happened. We are also looking for a way for the family to deal with its crises now and in the future. We thus need to keep track of the views of everyone in the family, including their language, metaphors, analogies, hopes, and dreams.

These views most often include the unwanted side effects of being traumatized, a wide variety of hardships and symptoms associated with PTSD, and the breakdown and dysfunction of the family system associated with adapting to traumatic circumstances. But they also include statements of hope, optimism, strength, pride, and courage that need to be supported, encouraged, and honored now and later on in the treatment program.

Once the problems are identified to the satisfaction of the therapist and the family (all family members who wish to be considered clients), we can move to the third phase of the treatment. This will be discussed in the next chapter.

## The Murray Family

The Murrays' initial therapy session following their assessment was the first time that family members had heard each other's unedited views about what was happening to the family. The parents talked about the pressures and pain they were enduring, much of which they attempted to hide from the children. This was surprising to the children. Though the mother and father were less surprised than their children about each other's experiences, it was useful information and helped them each appreciate why the other did as she or he did.

In turn and with more assistance, the children told of their difficulties in coping with the stressors inside and outside the home. The parents reported feeling both encouraged and discouraged by these reports. The father felt more depressed and ashamed after learning about the stress his children endured, partly because of his PTSD, yet he was glad that they were generally all right in spite of this and showed genuine love and respect for him. The mother felt a sense of incompetence, that she "should have known this anyway." Yet she too felt encouraged that the children were doing pretty well in spite of their pain and felt hopeful that things would get better now that everything was out in the open.

# seven

# **Phase III**

## Building Healing Skills

During the assessment phase you have developed a clear picture of the family's skills. Often it will be evident that the family are fairly skillful at relating to each other, at communicating important messages and ideas to one another, and at maintaining a balanced approach to family life that meets the needs of individual family members. In the case of families who have experienced catastrophic events, they may not know how to use their skills to deal with the extraordinary reactions they are having. In other words, their usual skills and abilities are just not sufficient for their current circumstances. Some families might have given up on some of their skills, since they were not successful at preventing the trauma from happening or at allowing the family to recover on their own. For other families you will have genuine concerns about the skill level you have observed.

Many individual trauma treatments that have been proven to be effective include a phase related to developing skills (Guerney, 1977; Kopp, 1982). Skills are introduced early in the treatment process so that the individual can rely on them in the later phases of treatment. In other words, these treatments are cumulative. Our model of family treatment uses the same principle.

In this chapter, we describe the skill development phase of family trauma treatment. We outline the rationale, strategies, and techniques for helping families either reinstitute or develop new skills around structure, relations, and coping. As with the other phases of our empowering approach, we support skill-building in areas that allow the family to heal successfully and deal effectively if presented with future traumatic circumstances.

## Building Skills Related to Family Structure

As described in Chapter six, family structure is an important aspect of family functioning and is impacted by the experience of trauma. In the sections below, we discuss skill-building strategies related to family structure, including rebuilding safety, re-establishing routines, and setting limits.

## Rebuilding Safety

Most experiences of trauma threaten people's sense of safety. Since a primary function of the family is protection, families often struggle post-trauma with how to restore safety. There are a number of techniques that can be used to help families.

Safety plans are often used in individual therapy, and this technique can be adapted for family therapy. Safety plans identify current threats and dangerous situations and outline the steps that can be taken to decrease the risk of harm. Families can develop safety plans by talking together about specific situations that do not feel safe and delineating the actions that each family member can take to reduce danger.

The Bissel family expressed continued concerns about family violence which occurs occasionally when their uncle and grandmother fight. This is a multi-generational family living situation. Living in the home are grandmother, her daughter, and her daughter's two children. Although the uncle does not live in the home, he comes around about once or twice a month. In the past during his visits, he has yelled obscenities at his mother, slapped her, and threatened her. After talking about this situation, the family agreed that it would be best if he not be allowed to visit or could only visit if the children were at school. The grandmother was willing to try to set some limits but felt as though she could not guarantee that her son would follow them. The family talked further about what they could do if he visited when the children were home. The family agreed that the children would go across the street and stay with their neighbor until he left. Mom also planned to call 911 if he started yelling. This plan was written down for the family to take home.

There are many families who feel they live in unsafe conditions. They may have safety concerns in their homes, communities, schools, and workplaces. Safety mapping is a therapeutic technique designed for such families. Safety mapping was developed as an activity for families participating in Strengthening Family Coping Resources (SFCR), an empirically supported multi-family group for families impacted by trauma (Kiser, 2008). It is also appropriate for use with families who are not participating in the multi-family group.

The goal of safety mapping is to help families identify when they do not feel safe and to develop strategies to increase their sense of safety. The family are seated around a table and are given a large sheet of paper or piece of poster board and pencils, pens, or markers. They are asked to work together to draw a picture of their house, street, and neighborhood and include the places they go on a regular basis. Once they have drawn their map, the family are asked to consider and mark places on their map where they feel safe and where they feel scared. They can use an informal rating scale from "very safe" to "very scared" to indicate how they feel at each location. If this map includes places where their trauma occurred they can indicate this as well. This will give the clinician an opportunity to educate the family about trauma reminders, and family members will be able to talk about places that trigger traumatic distress.

The second part of the safety mapping activity involves the family developing a routine that will increase their sense of safety as they go about their day. The family choose a place/time on their map when they feel scared. They talk about ways that they could change their routine that would support feeling safe. For example, a child in one family described feeling scared on the way to school in the morning. Older children in the neighborhood would bully her and she was afraid that they were going to hurt her. The family decided that the mom would walk the child to the bus stop and wait with her until the bus came in the morning.

## Re-Establishing Routines

An important aspect of family life is the performance of daily routines. But when something catastrophic happens, routines can be easily disrupted (Fiese & Wamboldt, 2000). One of the most effective ways to help families recover is to encourage them to re-establish daily routines as soon as possible (Kiser et al., 1998). Because of the trauma or the secondary stressors facing the family, the family may need to do some of their daily routines differently than before the trauma. Adjusting to changing routines can be uncomfortable.

The clinician can support this process by encouraging the family to think through what routines still work and what needs to be adjusted, to negotiate who will do what to carry out the new or modified routines, and to problem-solve about what could go wrong. As the family goes through this process, they are practicing many valuable skills, including defining roles and boundaries and proactive problem-solving.

Focusing on family mealtimes is an excellent way of helping families re-establish (or add healthy) routines in their daily life. The highly protective function of family mealtimes makes them an ideal target for family intervention following trauma (Fiese, 2006). Asking families to describe a typical family meal at their house is a good place to start. The good clinician will listen for how often the family actually share meals together, who prepares the meals, whether the family have some rules for their mealtimes (no television, no cell phones or other devices, everyone sits at the table), what the family talk about, and whether the family seem to enjoy this time. Using the family's description as the starting point, the therapist can help the family develop a healthy mealtime routine. Families should be asked to practice this routine by sharing at least one meal together during the next week.

## Reinforcing Rules and Limits

Structure in families is also established through rules and limit-setting. However, it is fairly common for families to relax or stop enforcing their rules and limits after they have experienced trauma. We often hear families say things like "We have been through so much" as a rationale for not maintaining reasonable rules and consequences. Often families, especially parents, simply need to be reminded about the purpose of rules and limits and the fact that everyone functions better when they realize that rules will be enforced fairly and consistently.

For other families, reinstituting rules and limits is more difficult. They will need to make a connection between their feelings of accountability and guilt over what happened and their lack of willingness to hold other family members accountable for their current actions. In this case, the clinician may need to help the family establish some temporary rules and consequences, and move to the next phase of treatment during which the family can process some of their beliefs about the trauma.

However, it is important that the family's distinctions between children and adults be honored. Thus, we always attempt to reinforce the authority of the parents by working through the parents to implement or carry out rules. If a child is violating the rules, for example, we expect the parent(s) to correct this situation (although we may remind the parent from time to time).

## Building Skills Related to Family Relations

### Developing New Rules and Family Communication Skills

Another skill-building focus in helping families frame the trauma and related problems is associated with introducing new rules for communicating within the family. To suggest that the family needs to develop new rules and skills of family communication too early in the helping process is counterproductive. However, at this phase in the treatment program the family may be ready.

You might gently point out to the family in their own language how impressed you have been at their success in reaching some resolution to the trauma and at how committed they are to ensuring that they not become incapacitated by a future trauma. Suggest, then, that part of their success may be due to the way they are talking with one another. Moving forward, however, the family will most likely be engaged in some tough conversations about issues they have found it very difficult to talk about, indeed issues that any family would find it hard to know how to discuss. The therapist might introduce the communication skill-building in the following manner:

> *Therapist:* Would you be interested in spending a session or two on some basic methods (rules and skills) for improving family communication? It might be a good idea to go over them and practice them between sessions as well. It would involve learning a couple of simple rules and skills and then, after you are doing well, putting them into practice in real-life conditions. Okay?

We try to focus on communication skills that will support the family's efforts to engage in the next phase of their trauma treatment, telling about the trauma and building a shared understanding of what happened and how the family can get past it. Some specific communication strategies will be useful.

One such rule is that "Anyone can speak about anything at any time as long as it is relevant to the focus of discussion and does not harm another person intentionally." Allowing everyone in the family an opportunity to speak about anything in front of everyone else in the family, including a stranger (therapist), often violates the unwritten rules of many families. This is particularly true for multiproblem families (H. McCubbin & Figley, 1983a). Clinicians must be sensitive to this variance, emphasize its importance, and be consistently supportive of those who attempt to follow this new rule, recognizing that it will be difficult.

Another important communication rule is that "Everyone in the family has a right to their own perspective on what happens and why things happen." Encouraging families to hear and appreciate differences in personal experience is critical. This is not a matter of what is factual; it is a matter of how we all view our experiences in idiosyncratic ways. So although families may outline the facts about events that happen to them, they need to acknowledge that there will most certainly be differences in opinions about how events are experienced. Families can practice adopting this new rule by talking about some mildly stressful events that they have experienced and giving everyone in the family an opportunity to voice their perspective.

Collaborative communication using a rule such as "No one voice in the family is the only voice heard and heeded" is necessary for the family to resolve difficult issues. Collaborative communication requires balancing power, influence, and control. Families will have to accept that the voice of some members is louder and carries more meaning—making authority than others (Besley, 2002). Their understanding of this dynamic though allows them to structure the family communication so that this is not the only voice heard. Families can make sure that all members express a point of view and that everyone's viewpoint is considered as they negotiate a shared meaning.

Paying attention to nonverbal as well as verbal communications can provide the family with additional information about how family members are feeling about issues being discussed. So a helpful communication rule might be "We watch what family members are doing as well as listen to what they are saying." Grown-up family members are probably much more attuned to messages communicated with words, while younger family members, especially young children, are often better communicators through gestures and nonverbal behavior.

## Strengthening Connections

### Sharing Positive Times

Family relations can be strained by the intense and primarily negative emotions that may predominate family interactions following exposure to trauma and high stress. A simple antidote is family fun and laughter.

Some families will need permission from the therapist to laugh and have fun. Especially if the trauma involved the loss of a family member, the family might believe that it is disrespectful to their missing family member if they enjoy some positive family moments. Additionally, families that blame themselves for the catastrophe may hold the opinion that they do not deserve to feel good. In these cases the therapist will need to make a powerful argument for why they are recommending that the family do some goofy and silly things.

Reminiscing about positive shared memories is one way to get the family started. The therapist can ask the family to tell a story about a time when they remember having a good time as a family or to talk about the last time that they had a good laugh together.

Again focusing on shared family mealtimes as an activity during which the family can enjoy some positive time together is helpful. Encouraging families to plan and carry out a mealtime each week during their treatment when the whole family (or almost everyone) can join together for some good food and meaningful conversation will improve family cohesion. Asking the family to practice their new rules of communication during the meal will help ensure a positive tone.

### Avoiding Blaming the Victim

Families will be unable to make much progress toward re-establishing interpersonal connections if their struggle to frame their situation is associated with blaming. There is a human tendency in dealing with highly stressful, particularly traumatizing, events to blame those most victimized (Figley, 1985b). This happens in the best of families with the most innocent of victims.

Frequently there is considerable animosity among family members toward the "victim." He or she is viewed, for example, as weak, unintelligent, incompetent, or unlucky. One of the goals of therapy is to enable family members to work through these feelings and, in the end, implicitly or explicitly communicate forgiveness of him or her. When this happens, the current situation shifts to individual family members becoming more responsible for their own fate. Also, it is easier to shift from a focus on the victim to the family system.

The story of the Wall family illustrates this tendency and a clinical method of dealing with it. Herb and Bonnie Wall sought help for their seventeen-year-old son, Ted, who was having trouble recovering emotionally from an auto accident. It became clear that both parents and Janet, Ted's nineteen-year-old sister, had not "forgiven" Ted for the accident, although they attempted to give the impression that they had. After sufficient information was collected, the therapist asked Ted a question:

> *Therapist:* Ted, what do you need from your family to help you recover from the accident?
> *Ted:* Forgiveness.
> *Mother:* Oh, Ted, how can you say that? We've given you everything. We've—
> *Ted:* Fine, thanks, but I feel you're disappointed in me, believe me—
> *Janet:* Why shouldn't we? It was a stupid thing to do—drink and drive, you—
> *Mother:* Janet! Stop picking on him.
> *Ted:* I don't want to be treated like a baby. Let me have it! I deserve it.

The therapist allowed the exchange to continue for a while and then asked everyone to level with Ted, and he with them. At the end of the session the family was asked not to talk about this matter again until the next session. Each family member was asked to write a two-page letter to Ted during this period (one week). On one side they were to tell him what they felt that was negative but didn't want to say until today, and on the other side they were to write what they felt that was positive. They were to describe their own feelings in the letter, to tell how it felt for them. Ted was asked to write on one side of the paper what he believed his family were trying to convey and on the other side what he believed they actually felt.

The next session was a lively and productive exchange that provided excellent material for the next phase of treatment. Briefly, the family tended to follow the same pattern of interaction established well before the traumatic event. This involved avoiding confrontation and disclosure of negative feelings, which, in turn, made others, in this case Ted, feel suspicious and frustrated about not knowing what was really going on. Ted and Janet were the only ones who apparently disclosed their true feelings in the exercise, though the mother and father made some progress. By the end of the session nearly all of Janet's points (that Ted showed "irresponsibility, immaturity, and poor judgment," among other things) were reluctantly endorsed by the parents. However, we were able to reframe these apparent victim-blaming statements into ones that emphasized behavioral rather than characterological faults. Moreover, these statements were accompanied with feelings of love, worry, and care for Ted by his family.

## Building Coping Skills

### Regulation

Families provide a sort of container for individual family members. Families define interactions that are appropriate by setting the rules and limits regarding acceptable expressions of emotions and behaviors. The definition of what is acceptable is set differently for every family. Some families are highly expressive, and yelling and boisterous interaction are the norm. In other families, quiet, careful expression is typical. In both of these kinds of families, when emotional and behavioral expressions are within this acceptable range, family members are comfortable and safe. The family feels regulated. What is acceptable can be altered by the experience of trauma.

It is usually helpful to have the family discuss their comfort zone. Sometimes the family will need to talk about their comfort zone before and after the traumatic event because it may have changed. If they can identify their comfort zone, then the therapist can ask them how it feels in the comfort zone. They can ascertain the intensity of feelings that is compatible with their comfort zone and talk about how to recognize the signs that family interaction is becoming dysregulated or moving out of the comfort zone.

Teaching families some simple regulation strategies is essential for families that are having difficulty with regulating affective interactions and behavior. We work with families to gain self-monitoring techniques and to practice ways to increase (up-regulate) or decrease (down-regulate) family affective expression and intensity.

Families who have experienced trauma often stop communicating and sharing. Because of the intensity of their emotional reactions and the risk for conflict (and even for violent exchanges), families members may withdraw or disengage from family interactions. This may be quite protective but may also be preventing the family from healing. During family therapy sessions, the therapist may observe family members shutting down or pulling away. Others in the family may not notice these silent cues. Reassuring the family of the safety of their interactions within the therapy session and encouraging all family members to engage in the process are critical.

Other families are concerned because the intensity of their interactions escalates rapidly and they feel out of control. We talk to these families about the autonomic nervous system. We note that part of the limbic system (i.e., mammalian or emotional brain) and the autonomic nervous system (ANS) with two branches (the sympathetic and the parasympathetic) regulates our body's response to stress of any sort (e.g., extremes in temperature, fear, joy) and is largely a set of involuntary processes. Because the ANS and its anatomical circuitry are so broadly dispersed, creating a general response, traumatic stress effects are felt throughout the body. We also note the physiological basis of the stress response—no matter the stressors—and how relaxation creates the opposite reaction to the stress response (Rothschild, 2000). Using a full grab bag of relaxation techniques, we teach the family multiple relaxation activities, making sure that they are developmentally appropriate for even the youngest members of the family. We usually cover deep breathing, progressive muscle relaxation, guided imagery, and mindfulness practices. We ask the family to choose a couple of strategies to practice. We help them structure a regular family relaxation time by identifying a time and place for the family to practice several times during the week (Kiser, 2008). Families usually gravitate fairly naturally to the relaxation technique that is most comfortable for them, and some favorites will quickly emerge.

## Planning and Problem-Solving

If the family has experienced trauma that was unpredictable and uncontrollable, they may feel discouraged about their ability to plan and problem-solve. They may believe that, if they were any good at it, they would have been able to prevent the trauma from happening in the first place. Even so, it is usually pretty easy for the therapist to persuade families that good planning and problem-solving are a good skill to have, especially for preventing future catastrophes from happening if at all possible. Deliberate planning and follow-through, which often require effective problem-solving, focus attention on the here and now (rather than the traumatic past, and may also provide an antidote to feelings of futurelessness), create a sense of efficacy, and provide opportunities for success (Folkman & Moskowitz, 2000; Kiser, 2007).

We introduce families to several methods for collaborative problem-solving, which we ask them to practice using real-life examples, including problems to which they are currently struggling to find good solutions. Common collaborative problem-solving techniques include negotiation, consensus seeking, and brainstorming.

We focus a good deal on preventive problem-solving (Kiser, 2008). As the family make plans, the therapist asks them to anticipate what could go wrong.

As they identify things that might get in the way, the therapist encourages them to consider how they might alter their plans to deal with potential problems.

## Building Social Support Within the Family

During the assessment phase the family's social supportiveness is discussed. If this is an area of concern for the family, further exploration of the family's sources of support and their ability to access and use these supports, especially under highly stressful or traumatic circumstances, is beneficial.

We begin with a discussion of social supportiveness, letting the family know about different forms of support and also about the benefits of both receiving and giving support. We talk about social support from an individual perspective, explaining how important it is for each family member to have people he or she can count on, emphasizing the need for supports within the family and outside the family. We also stress the importance of extended family, friends, and neighbors as a source of family support. Who does the family turn to when they need help or assistance?

Our discussion with the family highlights the extent to which family members seek each other out in times of need and, if they do so, an estimate of how satisfied they are with the support they receive. We like to inquire about multiple types of support, including emotional support, companionship, advice, tangible aid, and encouragement. We also talk with the family about who they rely on for support outside of their family.

Often the family's responses are a function of recent events that have severely damaged family relationships: trust, spontaneity, expressions of love, support, and encouragement, for example. Given violations in trust and safety, families often withdraw and risk becoming isolated from their supports, even from each other. This is part of the toll that trauma exposure can take on the family.

Sociograms are the charts or tools used to find the sociometry of a social space (Moreno, 1951) and are useful tools for working with families to identify their social support networks (Whittaker & Garbarino, 1983). In a family sociogram, the nuclear family (or the "family" as defined by its members) is the center circle. Extended family supports are listed in the next concentric circle, followed by neighborhood or community supports. The family is asked whom in each category they "turn to in times of need."

While the family completes the sociogram, we are looking for some consensus among family members regarding who goes in each concentric circle. We are also looking to see whether there are some family members who seem particularly disconnected from family social supports. If a child, for example, tends to rate a friend higher than any other family member, he or she can be asked in what ways her or his friend is more helpful or supportive than family members.

In cases where trauma has clearly interrupted social supports we may have the family fill out a sociogram thinking about their support network prior to trauma and contrast it to their current sociogram. This will provide an opportunity for the family to reflect on how the trauma has changed their family. This will be important information for the next phase of treatment.

With this information a therapist is able to determine how far the family needs to go to reach a minimum level of family supportiveness. With most families, family supportiveness increases naturally as family members are encouraged to talk with one another in supportive ways. However, the communication and interpersonal relatedness skills introduced directly affect supportiveness. Families can also discuss how to increase extended family and community supports and make specific plans for reaching out or for giving to others as ways to decrease their sense of isolation.

## Conclusion

Using our empowerment approach, this phase of the treatment ends with the family and clinician team confident that the family is equipped with the skills necessary for the next phase of treatment. Although the family may still feel some trepidation about moving forward and having frank discussions about their traumatic experiences, they can be assured of their ability to do so successfully.

# eight
# Phase IV
## Sharing and Healing[1]

Once the family has the necessary skills, Phase IV introduces therapeutic processes designed to help families actively address their specific traumas and related distress. This phase involves working with family members to reach some consensus about their experiences and, along the way, reframe their joint view in a way that makes their reactions more manageable and functional. There are three essential steps in the sharing and healing process: telling the trauma story, understanding the story, and building a healing theory.

We begin the chapter with a review of some of the roles and skills that the therapist will need to facilitate this phase.

> It is our hope, through this discussion, to give recognition to the complexity of this work and to provide some guideposts for those working with families who must attempt to bring each family member's experience of the trauma into alignment with the shared family story. (Kiser, Baumgardner, & Dorado, 2010, p. 246)

The foundation for Phase IV is narrative therapy.

Narrative therapy is a psychotherapy approach that was initially developed during the 1970s by Michael White and David Epston (1990). Today it is an accepted component of empirically supported treatment for individuals with traumatic stress disorders (Silverman et al., 2008; Wethington et al., 2008). Its origin, however, was within the field of family therapy (White, 1992). To our knowledge not until recently has this family trauma narrative process approach applied to families who have been traumatized. A family trauma narrative process brings members of a family together to share their trauma story. Kiser et al. (2010) suggest that the approach enables family clients to weave their trauma story (e.g., addressing the five victim questions), and their insights enable them to develop a healing theory about their circumstances. The family are able to develop a shared sense of meaning that is enhanced by improvements in family skills applied to, for example, problem-solving to minimize additional stressors.

Returning to the Family Adaptation to Trauma Model, we are attempting to get the family to revisit the trauma(s) (*T*) and related stressors (*S*) and secondary stressors (*SS*) by telling each other about their experiences and to reconsider how the *Family's Stress Reactions* were, in part, a consequence of *Family Perceptions and Processes*, often in the form of reframes. Sometimes these reframes or changes in perceptions happen suddenly and seemingly without the help of others—a kind of "aha" experience. At other times they are introduced among a number of other views and are repeated and built on throughout the narrative phase of treatment. Having completed the early phases in the treatment process, the family will have new regulation skills and new coping resources available during this phase. Families will learn as they struggle to adapt to the trauma that they have many critically important *Family Healing Resources* that also are part of the family's reactions, part of which can be helped by therapy, coaching, education, handouts, and simple reassurance.

## The Many Roles of the Therapist

Certainly, by now almost everyone has spoken some about their ordeal. But this phase of therapy involves collecting more detailed information about reactions to the traumatic event. This narrative process provides the critical building blocks for healing. And these elements will be extremely important in eventually building a family healing theory or explanation for what happened and why and in building a plan for dealing with future adversities as a family. This phase is probably one of the most difficult for the family and thus is demanding for the therapist.

The family trauma clinician using family-level trauma intervention must recognize developmental or experiential disparities among family members of various ages and work with the narrative skills of individual family members to co-construct a collective narrative. In addition, the therapist must monitor any dyssynchrony of family members' distress responses or courses of recovery (Pynoos et al., 1999) and emphasize emotional regulation, family communication, and meaning making (Kiser et al., 2010).

The therapist employs both theory and clinical experience when working with those creating a family trauma narrative. Even among clinicians experienced in narrative interventions, there is some debate regarding specific methods. For instance, clinicians differ on whether to encourage clients to retell details of their overwhelming experiences. Since trauma affects perspective taking and affect co-regulation (practicing characteristics) to the same extent as meaning making (representing characteristics), aiding families in strengthening their narrative skills and processes may be therapeutic in and of itself. Helping families build or adjust skills to adaptively create family narratives, instead of directly telling about traumatic events, may provide them with tools to cope with future stressors (Bohanek et al., 2006). However, among families who want to talk directly about their trauma, their discussions and ensuing shared story help them: to improve the memory of the event by re-establishing experiences, filling in missing details, and amending misinformation; to clarify interpretations and ascriptions; and to develop empathy for the pain inherent in the narrative (Kiser et al., 2010).

The precise approach to helping families reframe their traumatic experiences and associated thoughts and feelings will vary depending on both the family and the therapist. Similarly, families reach this phase of treatment at different points. Most of the families we have worked with begin this phase within the first two months of treatment, but some require much, much longer.

Families that tend to be ready more quickly than others appear to be the most functional ones. They are skilled in interpersonal relationships, enjoy each other's company, and genuinely like each other. The catastrophe they experienced undermined their faith not in each other but in nearly everything else. Many of these well-functioning families do not seek therapy and recover relying on their own resources. This does not suggest that they could not benefit from the help of a therapist, of course; they simply are able to use their own resources successfully. If they do seek treatment, they progress quite quickly through the five phases.

The families that take longer and find the process more challenging, however, were probably having problems—both individually and as a family—long before the catastrophe struck them. These families tend to have trouble reaching Phase IV and take longer in reframing their experiences toward a healing theory. Most of this chapter will focus on helping these types of families, because reframing does not come naturally for them.

It is the responsibility of the therapist to facilitate the family's collective decision-making about how to approach the trauma narrative. We advise that the therapist, in collaboration with the family as expert (Hester, 2004), begin by listing goals and defining rules and limits for the trauma narrative process. Identifying shared goals for the narrative work assures each family member of the importance of the effort involved. After developing such treatment goals, the therapist guides a family discussion about the narrative process, addressing: which trauma(s) to include; whether to provide details concerning specific trauma(s); how much detail to provide; whether all family members are cognizant of the details (s); and whether each member of the family has the necessary skills and is ready to participate. Once these choices are made, the clinician has a clearer understanding of when to probe for details and when not to, when to recommend concurrent individual therapy, and when to attend to how the family is narrating rather than what they are narrating (Kiser et al., 2010).

We begin the actual narrative phase of the trauma intervention with a review of stress inoculation practices (recently learned or reviewed by the family). This review acts as an essential antecedent and reminder of the shared duty of the therapist and caregiver(s) for regulating the narrative exposure so that it is not overwhelming. Otherwise, intense work may lead to emotional dysregulation and subsequent problematic externalizing and internalizing behaviors. Thus, as part of the intervention, the therapist must repeatedly monitor and promote co-regulation of family members, employing either down-regulating (i.e., calming, relaxing) or up-regulating (i.e., activating, energizing) techniques. When bringing each narrative session to a close, it is vital to ensure that each family member has attained a state of affective and behavioral control and is equipped to re-engage with life outside of therapy (Kiser et al., 2010).

Another key role of the therapist is monitoring explicit and implicit communication (as noted in Chapter seven). Typically, adults in the family focus on verbal communication; however, early elementary- and preschool-aged children frequently communicate nonverbally through play, gesture, or body language. Kiser et al. (2010) provide a clinical example to illustrate this: During one therapeutic exchange, a grandparent suggested that his grandson did not care about the family's traumatic experiences "since he never cried or showed any kind of sadness." The therapist then indicated that, during their discussion, the child had been playing with puzzle pieces and had formed several figures with sad or crying faces. Only after this therapeutic moment were the grandparent and young child able to appreciate the shared sadness they felt. In addition to monitoring expressive communication, therapists must also attend to the family's listening skills (e.g., synoptic, credulous, and empathic) as they narrate their story (Kiser et al., 2010).

## Telling the Trauma Story

The narrative is an opportunity for family members to tell how the traumatic event or catastrophe has affected them and their relationships with other family members. It also helps assure a more complete accounting of the past and current situation. With such an accounting the family is more prepared to develop a new, unified view of their trauma (i.e., a healing theory) that will guide their biopsychosocial recovery.

Memory management is the key ingredient in recovery from posttraumatic stress disorder. Thus, the therapist's task is to help family members recall the important information about the past; then it is necessary to help them collectively manage, restructure, and reframe this information.

Families are a marvelously complex system, owing, in part, to the fact that their members view the world differently from one another. There is no such thing as the family's view. This makes the task of memory management rather challenging, to say the least. There are at least two ways of accomplishing a family narrative, both leading to family members sharing important information about what happened to them.

The first method focuses on the stories of each individual family member. Rather simply, the first step is to urge everyone in the family to tell their whole story. From their perspective, what happened? What did they do during and following the most upsetting moments of the event? What were their feelings at these times? How are things now—better, worse, or the same? What are their hopes and fears for themselves and for their family?

It is extremely important to create a context that allows each family member to "tell her or his story," unabridged and unedited. This may be quite a challenge, since the views of one family member may be at direct variance to another's. Indeed, these conflicting views may in themselves be a major source of stress. Yet to tell one's version of the story in front of the family creates an opportunity to witness and appreciate the feelings and experiences of other family members.

Therapists should encourage each family member to articulate his or her experiences and feelings associated with the traumatic event in as much detail as possible. For example, therapists can encourage family members to talk about what kind of day it was when they first learned of the event, what they were wearing, and what they did and felt during and following their learning of the event. This will trigger new information, insights, and conclusions. For the entire family as well as the identified victim, this will reinforce the idea that the whole family was affected by the event and that the identified victim is important to everyone. In the process of disclosing the various views of the trauma and its aftermath, family members tap their own creative problem-solving resources.

As the individual family member's stories are told about how each experienced the traumatic event and its wake, a picture of the family trauma will emerge: for example, that all were quite upset and worried and tried to cope in their own ways. Which of these coping attempts helped or did not help? What efforts did more harm than good, compounding the stress for the traumatized person as well as other family members?

With new rules and skills for encouraging self-disclosures among all family members, therapists should reserve sufficient time to ensure that all family members talk about their feelings related to the trauma and its aftermath. This reinforces both the rules and the skills, and, more importantly, the hidden insights, feelings, and fears of all family members are more likely to be exposed and dealt with effectively.

Following is an example of what a therapist could say:

> *Therapist:* For the rest of our time today I would like each of you to describe what it was like when [use whatever language they use to describe the traumatic event and the posttraumatic period] happened to you. I want you to begin with the first moments right on up to right now. And it's important to allow whoever is telling their story to tell it completely and without interruption unless they ask for help in recalling something. Okay?
>
> *Mother:* Are you sure that the kids should hear all of this?
>
> *Therapist:* I'm sure. It's sensitive of you to be concerned about their feelings and reactions. But they are old enough to understand, and, from what they have said, I believe they want to understand what happened from your viewpoint. Is this correct or not, guys?

We do add one note of caution and often coach family members, especially parents, about sharing horrific or very frightening details of their trauma experiences. Sharing their stories is important, but so are the boundaries necessary for protecting family members from vicarious experiences of trauma.

Even though the traumatic event may have affected one family member more than another, as noted earlier *everyone* in the family experiences the trauma to some degree and is part of the recovery process. Each family member who is capable should be involved. Each is given an opportunity (and strongly urged) to describe in his or her own way the experiences, reactions, and views from his or her own perspective without editing.

It is often necessary to establish strict ground rules about interrupting another family member's story. If we do not do so, we risk restricting the amount and accuracy of what each family member will disclose.

The second method takes a coordinated narrative approach (Bohanek et al., 2006). Using this approach, the therapist simply asks the family to tell the story of what happened (again using whatever language they use to describe the traumatic event and the posttraumatic period). The family decides who will start. The therapist's role, in this instance, is to monitor the family's narrative process to make sure that everyone has ample opportunities to add, edit, disagree, or simply tell a different version. Following the family's lead is important but the therapist must be vigilant in encouraging less vocal members to speak up and share their versions, including their feelings about what happened to the family. The therapist might facilitate such exchanges by having whoever started the family narrative ask another family member how they remember what happened. In this method, the family narrative may seem, at times, more like a conversation among family members.

Regardless of the method used, these family sessions are frequently intense emotional experiences. Often these personal family member disclosures are extremely upsetting to other family members. This upset may be due simply to empathy, feeling bad for the suffering of this person, particularly a child. But it also may be associated with disclosing family secrets (for example, the father used drugs once, the mother had an affair, or an uncle molested a family member) or a point of view about the traumatic event that reflects poorly on another family member. The therapist must create a safe space in which the family is able to tolerate this intense experience. The therapist must also assure the family that this experience is critical to their healing.

## Understanding the Story

Empowering families to take control of their lives and future is the theme in this and the final phase of treatment. We have found that, in this phase of helping families deal with traumatic experiences, as they struggle to shape a healing theory, they should be given more and more control over the sessions, and the therapist's involvement becomes more that of a participant observer or facilitator. This involves assuming some of the responsibilities of a consultant: serving as a sounding board for other family members; being a person who is objective, clarifying, and encouraging.

Once the family have shared their story, the therapist, acting mainly as consultant, has a variety of strategies that can be used to help the family make sense of what happened. Moreover, in this mode of consultant, family members enable each other to propose a perspective about the trauma and its wake that fits for the family. Specifically, family members are encouraged to help other family members in (1) sharing perspectives, (2) listing consequences, (3) clarifying insights, (4) correcting distortions, (5) substituting new interpretations, and (6) finding new possibilities. Doing so assembles a sufficient set of building blocks for the family to build its healing theory, the final antidote to working through the traumatic event and being sufficiently prepared for future adversities.

## Sharing Perspectives

Family members are supported during the treatment sessions to assume (or reassume) responsibility for the skill of effective listening. They are assisted (through modeling and guidance) to gently help other family members view various situations from a different perspective. An objective of the family narrative process is for family members to recognize that there may be multiple realities and truths concerning the family trauma. This holds true even if all family members were present at the time of the traumatic event; each family member's individual experiences will be personal and unique.

> Our lives are multistoried. There are many stories occurring at the same time and different stories can be told about the same events. No single story can be free of ambiguity or contradiction and no single story can encapsulate or handle all the contingencies of life (Morgan, 2000). (Kiser et al., 2010, p. 247)

It is the role of the therapist to elicit the perspectives of each individual and then help integrate each perspective into a cohesive story (Kiser et al., 2010).

The therapist encourages the family to see each member as a partial knower and to come to appreciate multiple viewpoints through the give-and-take process of communicating and listening to the narrative. Understanding this concept can help bring the family together, improving family relations while simultaneously allowing room for individual growth (Kiser et al., 2010).

Kiser et al. (2010) provide a useful example: one child in a family at home during a house fire while a second child was not. The first child needs the other family members to hear and comprehend the details of the episode so that they can support him. This holds true even months later if he has not yet told anyone exactly what he experienced. The second child, on the other hand, may be overwhelmed by hearing the details; however, as he or she undoubtedly also experienced the secondary stressors associated with the trauma, the second child can provide a perspective that will likely be supportive of the healing process.

## Listing Wanted and Unwanted Consequences

In an effort to identify the full extent of the consequences of the traumatic event, each family member is encouraged to briefly (in five to eight minutes) talk about what the traumatic event means to him or her as a person and how his or her life has been disrupted. By assuring that these testimonials will be given and received in a positive way (rather than allowing them to lapse into a blaming session), the therapist assures the individuals that the experience will be quite productive. For example, nine-year-old Tim Murray disclosed: "I can't talk about my baseball game because Daddy keeps talking about the war."

The therapist asked at this point, "And how did that make you feel?" This helped the son identify the feelings he had related to these circumstances, and he went on to admit that his father's attention was very important to him but he understood that it takes time to feel better about something that was very scary.

The therapist might also find it helpful to get the family to construct a list of the wanted and unwanted consequences of the traumatic event. As the family begin to frame their situation, such a list is quite useful. Here it is especially important that everyone contributes to the summary list.

The antidote to bad memories and consequences caused by a traumatic event is the family's healing theory. In order to be effective, such a theory must include the few positive consequences of the traumatic event. These must be genuinely felt, not imposed by the therapist or only one family member.

The oldest daughter of a family of five was raped in her own dormitory bed at college. Friends with good intentions suggested that one positive outcome was that she had not been killed or needed hospitalization as a result of the attack. Though viewed as a positive outcome by others, the family saw it more as the absence of one more negative consequence.

There was one positive consequence that *was* listed by the family. Through the daughter's cooperation with the prosecutor's office, she was able to assist in the arrest and conviction of the rapist and thereby to prevent his raping again. Also, the attack brought the family closer together and, by doing so, or perhaps as a consequence, allowed the mother to disclose for the first time that she had been attacked as a teen by someone she had dated, but she had never told anyone until she told her daughter. The mother experienced great relief in telling her story, and the daughter felt a surge of empathy and acceptance of her suffering. It renewed their mother–daughter bond, which had been strained considerably through the teen years.

Another example of finding positive consequences occurred with a family whose only child, a two-year-old daughter, had been kidnapped for two weeks by a former babysitter. It had been two months since the child had been returned to them. Both parents had demanding professional careers that required them to rely on day care for their daughter. Both had taken a month's leave of absence and only now had sent their daughter, Candy, back to day care. They were both extremely upset about the ordeal and desperate for help in sorting out their feelings of anger toward the abductor, guilt about leaving Candy "unprotected," and anxiety about returning her to day care. They were also feeling unsupported by each other.

One of the most destructive facts of the trauma they were experiencing as a family was that they blamed each other and themselves for "putting careers ahead of children." This guilt played a major role in how they perceived the causes and consequences of their traumatic experience.

Gradually, however, they began to accept the fact that their careers were important to them personally as well as professionally, that their careers were a source of satisfaction and pride, and that the money and position they were earning would ensure that their daughter would have a good life. They slowly began to acknowledge that the kidnapping was a fluke that could not have been prevented. In the third session the husband summarized his position and that of his wife:

*Husband:* I don't think I'll ever trust anyone with her [daughter] again. There are some really strange people in this world, like the nutball who is now locked up [kidnapper]. And I don't think this distrust is bad, really. We know this thing could have happened to anyone. We're good and responsible parents. Maybe we will be even *better* parents now. We *know* what can happen, and we'll be taking extra precautions in the future.

## Clarifying Insights

We encourage family members to help each other clarify insights, perspectives, frameworks, and discoveries made by fellow family members by using the communication skills that they have practiced. We let them know that these new insights and perspectives will be essential later as they relate to constructing a healing theory or reframing some aspect of their experiences.

An example is the anguish felt when a ten-year-old daughter disclosed in session that she had been sexually molested by her father's brother five years earlier. The therapist turned to the father, who had made good progress in building his communication skills over the four weeks of therapy, and asked him to use his developing skills with his daughter.

*Therapist:* Dad, I would like you to turn your chair toward your daughter and ask her to tell you what happened. Use your listening skills and help her tell her difficult story.

What she told him no doubt was hard to hear. He later reported that it was difficult to concentrate on his daughter's feelings and experiences when he felt such rage toward his brother. Apart from his own feelings of inadequacy, anger, and frustration, however, he was able not only to clarify what his daughter was saying but also to express acceptance of her feelings and experiences. At the same time he was able to be as committed as he could to vindicating the situation and ensuring that this kind of victimization would never happen again to his daughter by anyone and that his brother would be prevented from doing this again, especially to his daughter.

But by concentrating on his daughter's story, the father was able to identify some critical insights and perspectives that would be critical to the family's healing theory several sessions later. She had indicated that she had grown up during those five years and had successfully resisted her uncle's advances and confronted him, and in the end he had apologized many times and vowed never to do such a thing again. The father's clarifications were just as good as mine:

*Father:* So what you are saying is your uncle was mean and bad and did things that made you feel bad. You were able to tell him "no" and make him stop. It seems like you are a very brave young woman.

The father later voiced skepticism about his brother's change of ways, but the family felt some degree of satisfaction in knowing that their daughter had worked things out well for herself. They continued to struggle with the fact that they were unaware of her struggles for so long, with the newfound problem with the uncle, and with the other challenges they faced.

We have found that families always possess the ingredients for coping with nearly all of their traumatic stressors. But listening carefully to what they say and feel and feeding this information back to them and helping them feed back to each other enable them to work through most of their traumatic experiences. Moreover, they are able to learn from their experiences so that they will feel more competent and confident about future challenges.

## Correcting Distortions

As noted earlier, traumatic stress treatment, or temporarily coping with traumatic stress, is memory management. Here the family members are encouraged to help each other "manage" the memories by correcting one member's distorted views or conclusions in a way that will lead to effective recovery. In addition, they also practice helping other family members to apply blame and credit objectively or fairly. This is a basic family relations skill. Some families are better at it than others.

The therapist's task is to praise any attempts by family members to shift attention from seeing only one victim in the family to viewing the entire family as being victimized. Family members should be encouraged (but not lectured) to examine the traumatic event that has disrupted family routine, to view themselves as having been deprived of the benefits of a normal family life as a result of the events and circumstances surrounding the trauma, and to rally together as a family to help each other overcome this trauma.

Narratives afford family members the joy of verbal mastery over what have in the past been traumatic memories of the event (Besley, 2002). Additionally, narratives allow family members to externalize the problems, challenges, or traumas they face. Kiser et al. (2010) have noted that the therapist works with the family to place the situation outside the individual or family, as if in a story. This is useful because it allows family members to observe the challenges from several different points of view. Another benefit of externalizing the situation is that it helps prevent blame and defensiveness while working through the trauma. Importantly, the narrative also provides family members with new ways to think about the trauma, allowing them to "mentally walk all around it and construct linguistically new ways of thinking about it" (Kiser et al., 2010, p. 247). Minuchin (1998) asks each member to notice the transactions and the patterns which create either constraint or freedom. Family members can no longer be afraid of discussing the past, fearing a blow-up among family members who disagree on the events. They can now discuss all aspects of the five victim questions and gradually gain control over their trauma memories.

An example of this is a family who have survived a car crash that permanently disabled the oldest child, Lissa, who was driving the family to a vacation spot. Prior to therapy the family focused exclusively on Lissa's trauma. Gradually, through a retelling of the events—both the crash and hospitalizations—the family began to recognize the challenges they face within each family member (e.g., guilt, responsibility, fear) and the mixture of anger about the accident happening in the first place, including Lissa's driving, counterbalanced with worry and love toward her.

This effort to modify distortions is much more powerful when it emerges from within the family system itself by both challenging and changing the original perceptions and equipping the family with powerful tools for managing future stressors.

## Substituting New Interpretations

Families often transform their trauma narratives by attending to details not noticed as important in the past. This approach, according to Morgan (2000), calls for strategic leadership by therapists: seeking to solicit additional circumstances that will enable clients to disentangle themselves from the influence of the traumatic event(s) and its effects. Within the milieu of narrative therapy, the narrative process is employed as a means to restructure the trauma story so that subsidiary story lines are drawn out. Therapists who utilize narrative interventions aim to draw out alternate stories which reveal acts of redress or endurance despite adversity (White, 2005). Moreover, through story reconstruction, narrative therapists aim to identify what family members find most meaningful, including values, hopes, and dreams (Morgan, 2000).

Often, the therapist who is mindful of unexplored parts of the narrative can ask questions designed to help the family contemplate the meanings and beliefs intrinsic to their story (Freedman & Combs, 1996; Levy, 2006). Speaking with the family about their evolving objectives and intentions, heroes who have affected them, turning points, or treasured memories may lead to unanticipated possibilities (Sween, 1998).

Similarly, family members are helped not only to "reframe" various perspectives about the trauma and its wake but also to connote positively what is currently viewed as negative. These new perspectives are the final major building blocks for constructing a healing theory for the family.

The Smith family illustrates substituting new interpretations. In the Smith family, the wife/mother was recovering from being raped by an intruder while the husband was away on business. The wife, when finally confronting the facts of the attack, concluded that had she screamed louder and fought harder she might have managed to avoid the attack. The husband, taking cues from the therapist, was able to gently point out that doing so might have caused the perpetrator to become violent and attack not only her but also their sleeping baby.

Initially the father/husband appeared to be more upset than anyone else. Gradually, he became more and more supportive. After suggesting that it would have been worse for his wife to have done anything other than what she had done, he proposed a totally different perspective for his wife to consider.

> *Therapist:* Mr. Smith, you mentioned just a few minutes ago that after you were able to calm down and deal with your own feelings of rage toward the attacker and guilt about not being there to protect your family, you mentioned in passing that Mom was kind of like a hero. Could you explain that?
>
> *Mr. Smith:* Yea, well it's just like . . . Well, if you think about this the way it *could* have worked out, it's amazing. I mean, the baby was unharmed, the whole thing lasted only ten minutes, and the rapist was arrested shortly afterward. All of this due to her—[facing his wife] your actions. You endured this creep in order to protect your family and to be sure he was caught and off the street. You're truly a hero! What guts!

It turned out that this little speech did more for the mother's recovery than anything else to help the family's recovery. For her it relieved any lingering guilt, assured her of the support and respect of her husband, and reinforced a growing sense of inner strength and confidence.

For the father, it was a lesson in humility (his wife was not a helpless waif and could cope well in emergencies) and reassurance that he could leave town and know things would be okay.

This "wife as hero" interpretation became the central core of what emerged as a very effective healing theory for the family, one that sustained them through the ordeal of helping prosecute the rapist and dealing with the lingering traumatic stress. It reassured them also that, irrespective of the coming life challenges, they were more prepared to face and cope with them.

## Finding New Possibilities

Lantz and Raiz (2003) have observed that an active therapeutic ingredient in constructing a trauma narrative is reworking the trauma. "Telling the story of the trauma pain allows the other family members to help you continue the story while changing the story line in a way that results in a better ending" (p. 169). The sting of the trauma can be removed by the family gaining a sense of mastery over the traumatic event by talking or playing out alternate endings, what they wished had happened or what they would have liked to have done differently. Pynoos, Steinberg, and Aronson (1997) describe these as "intervention fantasies" that "represent mental efforts to contend with or counter traumatic helplessness and injurious outcome" (p. 279).

Kiser et al. (2010) describe a case to illustrate how a family might work through their "intervention fantasies." In this case, a therapist encouraged family members to create multiple endings to their trauma narrative concerning the death of a family member during a domestic dispute. The victim's mother expressed a wish that she had known about the history of domestic violence so she could have convinced her daughter to end the relationship. The victim's sister changed the narrative ending by imagining that she had visited her sister's home that evening and had been able to prevent the dispute from spiraling out of control. Lastly, one of the victim's children speculated whether his sister could have saved their mother by phoning 911 when she called for assistance. Discussing these alternative endings allowed the victim's children to share details about the trauma that had not yet been disclosed and to talk about how afraid and powerless they had felt when their parents fought. This dialogue helped all the family members realize the extent to which they wished they could have prevented the victim's death, providing them with a path to support each other in working through their burden.

Problem-solving and implementing new coping skills are considered key components of trauma treatment (Lantz & Gyamerah, 2002; Salmon & Bryant, 2002), and the narrative process may enhance the development of these competencies. According to Angell, Dennis, and Dumain (1998), "Story alterations offer potential therapeutic changes because shifts in the story alter the teller's experience of the world. Changes in the story provide access to new solutions" (p. 623).

## Building a Healing Theory

Now that the family has generated the various thoughts and feelings about the trauma, the task is to reframe and assemble these views into various compatible components of a "healing theory." Also, there is a concerted effort to directly face any and all posttraumatic symptoms and reframe them in order to make them more manageable and more directly linked to the recovery process.

Formed from the collection of family members' stories and theories, the family may begin to build a family healing theory. It emerges as a kind of antidote to the ordeal suffered by the family to date and will sustain their recovery into the future. Moreover, an effective healing theory helps in preparing the family for future traumatic events and, by doing so, enables them to avoid a good deal of unwanted consequences. It addresses the fundamental questions that all trauma victims attempt to answer in an effort to recover emotionally from their ordeal.

But you might ask why we call this a "healing theory." It relates to the concept of "trauma" as a wound. A theory, as defined by any standard dictionary, means "an analysis of a set of facts in their relation to one another; a belief, policy, or procedures proposed for following as the basis of action; an ideal or hypothetical set of facts, principles, or circumstances." To "heal" a wound or trauma, we need a theory or belief, set of principles, or hypothesis that enables us to pose and answer the five victim questions.

In the previous phase the family members began to reframe various facets of their traumatic event and current circumstances. They began to reach a general consensus regarding the building blocks for a healing theory, a set of new perspectives offered by various family members. These collective reframes were proposed in part by various family members and are important pieces of a family healing theory. Developing this healing theory emerges at this phase of treatment by building on the observations and perceptions of family members that have emerged over the past several treatment sessions.

We have found that, to be effective in building a healing theory, it is necessary to help and encourage each family member to work cooperatively and to show signs of insight and acceptance of the current crisis and optimism about handling this and future challenges throughout the last phases.

Finally, it is necessary to begin to guide the family to articulate the full meaning of the trauma and its wake. This is done by asking the family to address each of the victim questions: What happened? Why did it happen? Why did we act as we did throughout this ordeal? Why are we acting as we are right now? If something equally challenging happens in the future, will we cope better?

As each family member discloses his or her précis, other family members frequently ask for clarification or justification. In the end, the family settles on a consensus view or healing theory about the traumatic event and its impact on the family. Let us review each of these fundamental victim questions in order to emphasize their importance and that the answers must emerge gradually from the family members themselves separately and for the family system collectively.

## What Happened?

The fundamental issue for everyone faced with a stressful situation—be it pleasant or unpleasant—is attempting to fully grasp specifically what took place. With sufficient information we then can categorize the event-threatening, nonthreatening, controllable, or uncontrollable—and immediately deal with the next fundamental question: "Why?" Often, however, we revise our initial assessment of what happened. We begin, for example, from our own perspective and quickly realize that more people are affected than just ourselves.

An example of this is the process by which an American hostage held against his will by a terrorist group revised his perspective of what happened.

> *Hostage/victim:* Initially, I concluded that I was held hostage by a terrorist group for twenty-three days, that during this period I was deprived of my freedom, confined to a small room with my hands and feet chained, fed poor food and water, with no opportunities for exercise. I escaped and had to endure three days in the jungle until I was found by a local family. I was then subjected to humiliating interrogation by both the host country and U.S. State Department officials. I was reunited with my family in the capital city without any recognition of or compensation for my suffering.
>
> Later I began to realize that my family psychologically suffered in this ordeal as much as I, since I knew what was happening and they didn't. They had to endure the unknown, various false rumors of my death, my premature release, and my culpability as "drug runner."
>
> *Therapist:* How was it for them?
>
> *Hostage victim:* After we were reunited, I expected them to be exactly the same as they were when I left them, but they were not. They were traumatized and frantic. And they expected me to be not at all the same: traumatized and frantic. Yet, by the time we were united, I had regained my composure, was able to get cleaned up, and had had a good night of sleep.
>
> ... Finally, I began to see that we as a family were victims—all of us—of some very nasty people. But we are in relatively good shape psychologically.

## Why Did It Happen?

Another fundamental question is "Why?" This, of course, is more difficult to answer. This is a critical question for making meaning from the experience of trauma, although for some there is no acceptable answer.

For some, faith, spiritual beliefs, and religion may provide answers. Although explicit explanations are important, particularly in being more prepared to avoid such situations, faith in knowing that the traumatic event was due to some divine will or plan is very comforting to some. Yet what works for one person may not be so useful to others, even in the same family. Thus, as a family struggle to search for explanations for why such things could affect them and not others, one family member's explanation may be another's annoyance.

There was the case of a family grieving over the death of a child. The couple sought marital therapy associated with sexual and communication problems. The first anniversary of their child's funeral was in a few months. In the second session, which focused on their marital communication system, the wife began to focus on the tragedy. It became clear that part of the problem was that there was little consensus about why it had happened. Both agreed about the critical components of the event: the child fell into a neighbor's pool after maneuvering both a locked door and a fence. The husband leaned on his belief that it was "God's will." This explanation was not only unacceptable to the wife but was also part of the reason why she felt betrayed by her husband, unsupported in her efforts to recover from the grief because, as her husband suggested, her "faith was not strong enough to trust in God's will and move on."

Between sessions the therapist wrote a brief note to the couple, which said, in part:

> The emotional pain you both feel for your son is real and equally distributed. Losing a child, especially one like Phil, is the most difficult loss imaginable. You have both coped as best you could. For now, John, you have found comfort in your faith; Jane, you have not. It is reasonable to conclude that this pain and these differences are connected with your marital problems. It is now time to cope as a couple, as a marriage. For the next session I would like you each to pretend to adopt your spouse's point of view in coping with the death of Phil. I am very serious, and I want you both to be serious about this task. Call me if you have any questions.

The task worked effectively. Each was able to see the other's point of view and appreciate the need for a common view to emerge. Such a view evolved within the following two sessions. This view, which was to be the central core of their healing theory, could be characterized as follows:

> We loved Phil very, very much. The accident was beyond our control, and no one can be blamed. Because we loved him so during his life, it takes a very long time to accept the fact that there *is* no explanation for his death other than circumstances. All we can do is have faith in God's help and guidance in moving on with our lives and the hope that we shall be blessed with another child who we can love.

## Why Did We Act as We Did During the Catastrophe?

The third victim question involves both culpability and coping behavior. Often our view of the way we reacted to a traumatic event is as troubling as the event itself. Moreover, our actions and reactions during a traumatic event make sense only on reflection, months or years later. Through this perspective we are able not only to answer this fundamental question but also to evaluate our behavior in proper perspective. We can recognize that we were attempting to cope with extraordinary circumstances (for some, a once-in-a-lifetime challenge) that would stress and overwhelm nearly anyone. Finally, by viewing our behavior (for example, symptoms of PTSD) in this broader perspective, we are given more hope that the unwanted reactions, behaviors, and symptoms will disappear as we recover from the trauma.

The task is more complicated within the context of the family. We must not only understand and accept our own actions during the traumatic event; we must do likewise with fellow family members. Families coping with trauma often focus first on simple survival; family members may behave out of character: rude, violent, petty, jealous, frightened, cold, rejecting, or short-tempered.

In attempting to account for our own behavior, we also need an accounting of the behaviors of others. With this we can place the reactions of the family, as a group, in proper perspective and, as a result, understand these reactions, accept them, and, if needed, forgive them.

## Why Have We Reacted as We Have Since the Catastrophe?

Just as we tend to struggle to understand what happened at the time of the traumatic event, we are often perplexed at our actions and feelings following the event. Those exposed to highly stressful events are often dismayed by their inability to "forget about it and go on with life." Moreover, friends and family— and some professionals as well—slowly begin to promote this method of overcoming the traumatic memories. These unsuccessful efforts to manage memories—be it through attempting to forget or constantly ruminating about them—tend to undermine even further the victim's self-concept and self-confidence.

What is important at this point in the recovery process is for victims—all family members—to become accepting about the immediate and long-term biopsychosocial process of recovering from traumatic stress. We must assure our clients that their actions are completely normal and predictable reactions to an abnormal and unpredictable set of events.

Irrespective of the functionality of the client family, most experience numerous troubling symptoms. These symptoms include but are not limited to those described in Chapter two: startle responses, difficulty falling asleep, staying asleep, nightmares, flashbacks, guilt, depression, apathy, and relationship difficulties such as increased conflict, suspiciousness, and overprotectiveness.

Moreover, other problems emerge as the family attempt to cope with the traumatic and associated stress reactions—for example, a family attempting to overcome the hardship of losing a home and two pets to fire. As their home was being rebuilt they lived in two large rooms at a local hotel. During this period the family experienced a series of conflicts associated with disciplining their children, watching television, and general signs of dislike and anger shown to each other in addition to some of the symptoms noted above. The family needed to view their current difficulties in the proper perspective (reframe) that they would not be exhibiting most of these symptoms and hardships were it not for the fire.

So posttraumatic symptoms—both individual and systemic—are, of course, quite normal but are extremely upsetting to the family. In helping the family recognize and face these symptoms, it is important to help the family members reframe each symptom.

As noted in the previous chapter, the therapist should attempt to "normalize the presenting symptoms" as much as possible and emphasize that, indeed, displaying these symptoms is a good sign. Such symptoms are an indication that the nature of the family's problem stems from the traumatic event and is much more amenable to treatment than, for example, a faulty family system.

Yet, from the enormous research that has been conducted focusing on the personal and interpersonal reactions to traumatic events, we know that there is considerable overlap in the symptoms experienced by family members and by families. Table 8.1 lists some common symptoms, the most frequent meanings assigned to them by families, and suggested reframes, which may or may not fit a particular family but can be modified by the therapist to do so. This list illustrates the opportunity of the therapist to help the family reframe or "positively connote" what has been perceived as negative for so long. Obviously, every case is unique, and it is critical that the therapist match the reframe to the family's own situation, language, metaphors, and pacing.

Returning to the case of the family dealing with the kidnapping of their daughter, a turning point came when both parents realized that they had different stress management styles. What the wife initially viewed as a demonstration of her husband's lack of love for her and insensitivity to her feelings was replaced by a view of him as someone who had always had difficulty with feelings. She recalled, partly through the traumagram, other times in their marriage in which disaster struck and her husband, in her words, "turned into a computer."

*Wife:* I now see that he loves my daughter and me very much and wants to be supportive. He's just never learned how to do so. His way of coping is to roll up into a ball, emotionally, and hide. It's nothing against me. So when I see this happen in the future, I will know that he is having trouble coping, too, and not to expect him to respond as I do.

**TABLE 8.1.** Old and New Interpretations of Common Symptoms

| Symptom | Family's Perception | Reframed |
| --- | --- | --- |
| Flashbacks | Haunted by the past, indicator of mental illness, lifelong problem | Vivid recall ability, useful indicator of "trauma work" needed |
| Depression | Giving up, withdrawing, selfishness, weakness | Taking a break to recuperate, not wanting to be a burden to others |
| Guilt | Poor self-concept or self-esteem, errors in judgment or actions | Courage, self-responsibility, selflessness, kindness, humanness |
| Substance abuse | Weakness, self-indulgence, hopelessness, impulsiveness | Effort at self-help, avoiding being a burden, need for support |
| Acting-out child | Presenting problem, disrespect for parents' authority, poor discipline | Effort to bring attention to needs of family, sign of love, concern |
| Family conflict | Sign of poor family health, lack of support, family not going to make it | Sign of stress that would affect *any* family, not on same team yet |
| Family stop talking to each other | We can't talk about "it," sign of poor communication skills, sign of relationship problems | Normal avoidance and numbing, did not have the skills necessary but now they do |

## What If Something Like This Happens Again?

Another way of posing this question is: "If something equally challenging happens in the future, will we cope better?" This question also considers the issue of faith, be it faith in God, one's self, one's family, or all of these. The answer we develop builds on the answers to the other victim questions.

Often we ruminate about the prospects of the same traumatic event occurring again. Even if we are reassured that it no doubt will not happen again, the remote possibility motivates us to think through our course of action. In doing so, then, we may analyze our previous actions and work out more effective strategies. Discussing the contingencies, irrespective of the emergence of a final plan of action, and reaching a general consensus about handling future catastrophes is extremely reassuring to families, and having such a plan is one more sign that they are no longer traumatized—they have recovered from the catastrophe, and they are in control.

Beyond figuring out how the family might react differently if a similar trauma happened to them again, we want the family to know that they have developed new strengths (skills, insights, understandings, and ways of supporting each other) that would serve them well if they were confronted with additional traumas. The family's belief in their ability to cope effectively with whatever comes their way is a powerful antidote to their feelings of hopelessness and futurelessness.

Together, all of the answers to these fundamental victim questions, in addition to the many insights and new perspectives emerging among family members, can lead to a useful first draft of a family healing theory to cope with and eliminate their traumatic stress. Although it might be useful for you to outline the healing theory, for it to be most useful at least one family member must be able to describe it.

Families struggling to overcome traumatic distress often attempt to rush to reach closure or consensus about a healing theory. A well-intentioned outsider, professional, friend, or outside family member may urge the family to adopt some pat explanation (for example, "God's will" or "it could have been worse") and put the experience behind them. Most often those who suggest these shortcuts feel uneasy with the family when traumatic memories are discussed. When someone says "Put those bad memories behind you," that person is actually saying "Hide those bad memories from me."

But even with traumatized families who are proceeding in therapy and working to develop a healing theory, the process can be rushed and, as a result, be ineffective in helping the family work through their traumatic experiences. Sometimes a therapist or family member may become impatient with the progress of treatment. However, we have learned the hard way that imposing a reframe on clients before they are ready or imposing one that they do not agree with can be disastrous. Rather than rush the process, the therapist must learn to listen very carefully to family members and wait for *them* to offer alternative perspectives. At these times, it is critical to slow down the process of consensus building (regarding the healing theory) and make sure everyone agrees. It might be necessary to go over the scenario several times to reach a point in which there appear to be no additions or corrections. Each family member must clearly be satisfied with the view.

It is not necessary for all members of the family to adopt the family theory with equal amounts of enthusiasm. Indeed, the children may not be as aware as the adults about the details and may even be somewhat skeptical about some aspects of the theory. What is important, however, is that everyone in the family believes that the family healing theory is a good working draft and will be acceptable until another is offered and accepted, and that it is sufficient to keep the peace and get back to functioning like a whole family again.

Often the family's healing theory will lead the family to discover that they need or want to take some action to mark the trauma or the changes the family have gone through. Attaching action to their healing theory allows them to incorporate some symbolism and ritual into their healing process. It reinforces their understanding, brings a sense of resolution, and supports their forward movement. Helping the family plan and carry out this activity often brings an end to this phase of the treatment process.

## Conclusion

What we try to do in this phase, then, is to encourage the client family to reconsider the circumstances. We gently try to get them to reexamine various thoughts and feelings about the trauma and its consequences and to reframe them and, thus, the problems or challenges they face. This means that the family discover or are introduced to an array of perceptions about their predicament that includes a view that is more tolerable and adaptable for family functioning.

Indeed, at least one of these perceptions includes the basic ingredients for a healing theory for the family in coping with their particular traumatic situation. Like any theory, a family healing theory contains a set of propositions, principles, and assumptions about a particular situation. Such a theory is useful in both explaining the current predicament and predicting future outcomes.

We are suggesting that such a theory can emerge naturally in most highly functional healthy families. Yet even the most dysfunctional traumatized family can be helped to create such a theory through the guidance of a skilled therapist. It emerges in the process of a continuing discussion among family members.

Though less elegant than most scientific theories, a family's healing theory provides a semantic antidote or medicine for treating and "curing" the trauma "infecting" the family system.

## The Murray Family

In the case of the Murrays, Mr. Murray revealed that his wife began to avoid talking with him more and more by going to bed and getting up before him. He believed that this was an indication of her not wanting him to talk about his painful war experiences. He slowly began to see that there was another explanation. She felt like a failure as a wife because she was unable to help him work through his trauma. Each time he brought up the war or displayed symptoms of PTSD, it was a reminder of her failure. With the therapist's help, he began to reframe his perception of her behavior from a sign of rejection to a sign of love.

Eventually, the entire family began to recognize that what they once saw as a tragedy and a terrible burden was a challenge and that they could work together to overcome it. They began to realize that working through this crisis together made them better equipped as a family to deal with future adversities.

Moreover, for the Murray family, the potential existed to reframe the "problem" of Tammy's suicide threat into the possibility that she was desperately attempting to save her family through self-sacrifice, to bring attention to herself to highlight the challenges faced by other family members during the past several weeks. This "self-sacrifice" was a sign of love and concern in a desperate appeal for help for the people she loved.

The reactions of her brother and parents were indicators that they loved and cared for her welfare. The family discovered that it was out of her love for them that she considered sacrificing her own life. This new "reframing" of the problem allowed each family member to reconsider the current situation. They were interested in ensuring not only that Tammy did not commit suicide but also that the family's pressures and stressors were identified and managed effectively.

To make this effort more concrete, perhaps another example from a therapy session with the Murrays might be helpful. In this phase, after each family member had described the ordeal from her or his perspective, the therapist needed both to summarize the progress made so far and to help the family shift their attention to developing a healing theory by beginning to reframe certain key factors, to see things from a different, more constructive perspective.

Specifically with regard to reframing the trauma, the dialogue might have been:

> *Therapist:* I am very impressed with all of you. You have told your stories well, and the others have been very supportive. I would like to ask you all to now help me try to make sense out of all of these views by first identifying the things everyone agrees on and then dealing with the others in the order consensus (most to least). Okay? Who would like to start?

The mother raises her hand and everyone directs their attention to her.

> *Mother:* Well, it seems like all of us wished that this whole thing had never happened [laughs from several family members]. But another thing was that it has brought us together; we're closer now, and we trust God's judgment more than ever; our love for one another is stronger than ever [everyone nods their head].
>
> *Father:* On the negative side, I think that everyone thinks that I should have gotten some help for my Vietnam stuff a long time ago.
>
> *Mother:* I don't agree, because I don't think you knew what was happening to you and wouldn't have known where to go for help if you did [everyone nods their head].

This discussion continued until the family was able to list a number of things in which there was complete agreement. The nightmares and more controversial issues (often between children and parents) had to be negotiated by the therapist and were generally issues that went beyond the traumatic event. One issue, for example, was the autonomy of the daughter. She felt that her parents were restricting her freedom because of the suicide talk. Her parents emphasized that her freedom had been an issue for over a year, long before the traumatic events began to emerge. It was partially resolved by a compromise perspective: that the parents had become even more cautious about her behavior outside the home and increased parental supervision, but that this might change if treatment were successful (that is, symptoms would go away and calm be restored).

The healing theory for the Murrays incorporated the family's new understandings about the imposed injustices of postwar emotional adjustment endured by the father, the pressures of dual-career families, and the extraordinary stressors of children, culminating in a display of love and caring within the family system.

The Murray family's healing theory emerged as the consensus view of all its members. The mother was the first to put it all together. Her first attempt was altered by nearly everyone in the family, although more in form than in substance. This third "draft" was adopted by everyone.

> *Mother:* We love Tammy very much. Although she really didn't want to commit suicide, her talking about it made us notice her sadness and, in turn, the sadness and upset of all of us in the family. Through these family sessions we realize that many of these problems began soon after Dad started having problems related to the war. We love Dad very much, and his becoming upset about the war made us realize how important he is to all of us: as father, husband, and friend. At first he seemed angry and depressed, and we blamed ourselves. We thought he was mad at us, wanted us to go away. We were afraid he was trying to tell us that he wanted to move out. Now we know that the memories of the war and his experiences as a corpsman had always bothered him and that only now was he ready to finally deal with them. It took him and us a while to figure out what was happening. We tried in our own ways to help. Most of the time we did not help because something like this has never happened before. We now see that these attempts, though unsuccessful, were signs of love and caring. We now see that Dad was bothered by the war because he is a kind and sensitive man who endured a very scary and depressing time. He now understands why he has acted as he has since the war and knows what to do if he has bad feelings about the war again. We have grown closer as a family because of this situation. We are stronger and tougher than ever and not only can deal with any other problems that might happen in the future but also can be helpful to other families who might become overwhelmed as we were. We are survivors!

For the Murrays and for most other families, discovering and effectively articulating a healing theory are the climax of a successful treatment program. Yet there is one more very important phase. Just as the reader of a great novel or viewer of a great movie may become dissatisfied with a poor ending, a fine and successful therapy program can become less so with an ineffective termination. This is the focus of the next chapter.

## Note

1  Because of this chapter's overlap on family story and narrative processes with Kiser, Baumgardner, and Dorado (2010), we have borrowed heavily from this paper for the chapter.

# nine

# **Phase V**

## Moving Forward

## Closure and Preparedness

As family members have increased their effectiveness in coping in general and begun to articulate their healing theory and negotiate its precise conceptualization, they enter the final phase of treatment, closure and preparedness. Over the course of this empowerment intervention, the need for therapy becomes less and less obvious. You have, in effect, worked yourself out of a job!

This simply means that the family should be terminated as clients in an effective and responsible manner so that: (1) they recognize that the goals of therapy have been reached, (2) they can feel a sense of accomplishment for their recovery, (3) the therapist shifts from being their full-time therapist helping them reach a specific set of objectives to being a resource who can be called on at any time in the future, (4) they will be as prepared as possible to deal with future stressors, and (5) their program of treatment will be reinforced through contact with others similarly affected. As with the previous phases of our treatment program, this phase may begin soon after the family begins to articulate a healing theory and may last from one to six sessions. Every family is different with regard to how they welcome or avoid therapy termination.

## Reaching Treatment Goals

At this stage in the treatment model with families there should be an emphasis on reviewing the goals that were jointly established initially and helping the family determine how well they have achieved these goals. This involves five components: (1) reviewing where the family started; (2) reviewing what they have done in treatment—what they have learned and how they have changed; (3) deciding whether and how to measure their progress; (4) redoing some parts of the initial assessment to compare results; and (5) considering whether during that change process new issues or concerns have emerged and, if so, whether the family now have the tools and skills (new or old) to deal with these new challenges effectively.

Returning to the Family Adaptation to Trauma Model, we want to determine where the family is on the model and in their process of adaptation. We do so by assessing whether the family's *Current Stressor Context* is more manageable, their *Perceptions* are more reality-based, more consensus-driven, and healthier, their repertoire of *Healing Resources* has been replenished and/or new resources have been added, and their *Trauma Reaction* is not causing distress. As the family review their current level of adaptation, they have likely returned to pre-trauma functioning or are now thriving.

We have found it important during this phase to reassess the family using the battery of instruments they completed earlier. This testing will provide additional data for determining the effectiveness of therapy and the need for follow-up. Moreover, if there appears to be some prospect of the family's being exposed to greater stress in the coming year, there may be some regression effects. If so, these same instruments should also be administered between six and twelve months following therapy and the family be invited to participate in one or two follow-up sessions.

## Sense of Accomplishment

It is hard for some families to feel a sense of accomplishment in their struggles to overcome a traumatic event. Many report long periods of feeling "numb" and near-amnesia. It is not surprising because, as was noted in the first several chapters, families are often overwhelmed with traumatic and posttraumatic stress, in addition to their everyday stressors and pressures. It may be quite clear to the therapist that the client family have reached the treatment goals and objectives. The family may not share the therapist's sense of accomplishment. They may feel unprepared or not as they were prior to the traumatic experiences, or they may have become dependent on the therapist or therapy. In such cases we have found it useful to place the family's current functioning in proper perspective, contrasting it with the pretreatment period of crisis and confusion.

Consider, for example, the case of a mother of three who had been widowed two years prior to treatment as a result of an auto accident and had not remarried. She had sought out help for her oldest (twelve-year-old) child, who was having difficulty in school. It was clear that the mother was overwhelmed with pressures, only some of which were associated with the grief over her husband's death. As the individual family members dealt with their grief and their new life stressors, their family relations became strained. During the final session the therapist played a videotape of the first session to illustrate for the family just how far they had come and how much better they were getting along.

Although the tape had been made only two months earlier, at that time the mother had looked years older, had trouble concentrating, was easily startled, and had difficulty understanding her children's perspectives. All this was evident to her toward the *end* of therapy. She recognized similar improvements in her children. This in addition to recognizing her achievements on each of the therapy goals reinforced her sense of accomplishment.

> *Therapist:* You know that you and the children were able to work through the stressors in your life and finally bury your husband. You did it, not me. You have taught me the meaning of courage, insight, fortitude, and humility. This does not mean that you won't have setbacks in the coming months; I would be shocked if you didn't. But you need to at least pause for a while and note how far you have come.

## Transition Therapist to Resource

The nature of the therapist's role shifts from that of a major to a minor player in the family's gradual recovery process. Contact with the client family becomes less and less frequent, eventually reduced to periodic phone calls or a letter of inquiry about their recovery progress.

As family clinicians and training supervisors for many years, we have found that the end of therapy is different for the client family and the therapist. It is a challenge for both but for different reasons and often harder for the therapist.

## Family Therapist Challenges

The reason why concluding (terminating) a case is one of the hardest tasks for family clinicians is timing: making the decision to bring it up. We like the analogy of dancing with someone at a bar in which the music never stops. After the third song you have had enough but think your dance partner may wish to continue, not knowing that he or she felt the same. Clients assume that the therapist will inform them when the "dance is over." And some therapists make the same assumption about their clients.

The therapist must make the call, and when clients know that therapy includes various phases, such as the ones described in this book, they are

prepared for the final phase. Moreover, an intervention program that emphasizes concrete goals and objectives suggests, by definition, the appropriate end
point for the program, when the objectives are reached.

Ending the dance and saying good-bye to clients is especially difficult for a
beginning therapist, more than for a client family, particularly one that appears
to have reached the clinical objectives and appear "healed." Thus, our observations here are more for beginners than for the more experienced family
trauma therapists.

One of the biggest problems for beginning therapists is to let clients go or,
conversely, to allow clients to let go of them. Good therapy is like a good movie:
it is over before we know it, and a part of us wants it never to end. Sometimes
we need to have a "The End" sign for our clients. But some movies end too
abruptly, and we feel cheated and frustrated. Our clients need to see their
progress and be aware that the end of full-time, intensive therapy is associated
with reaching the specific clinical objectives.

The therapist may wish to continue the sessions because, although there are
signs of completion, the therapist (1) enjoys this case for one or more reasons,
(2) believes that the clients need more therapy, (3) does not know how to
terminate in an acceptable way, or (4) two or all of the above.

Some clients, aware that the end is near, experience a relapse: worsening or
redevelopment of the presenting symptoms or experiencing new problems that
require attention in session. This kind of "slippage" is quite normal in families
struggling with significant change in their interpersonal relationships, and the
therapist needs to convey this to them. Indeed, the therapist can forecast this
and warn them that this will happen. However, this may also be an indication
that the family are finally willing to focus on deeper, more troublesome
problems. Only now are they emerging, perhaps out of the family's fear that
they will not be resolved if therapy is terminated. It takes years of practice for
therapists to make that differentiation.

## Challenges of Family Clients

An experienced family therapist, however, can also pick up certain cues from
client families that the end of therapy is going too fast. Families may fear that
changing their routine of coming to therapy each week may be harmful, that
they have come to rely on these times as a means of focusing on marriage,
family, and parental issues, or that they have become dependent on the
therapist's contributions as a family member. This too is perfectly normal,
particularly with families who have experienced trauma. For these families the
shift in the therapist's role needs to be more subtle and gradual. For example,
the therapist can gradually turn the session leadership over to the parents and
simply begin and end the session and contribute something only when it is

vital. Changing the day or at least the time, if not increasing the time between sessions, is another way of gradually shifting the dependency of the family. Irrespective of the method, testing the results of these shifts provides a good indicator of the family's receptivity to terminating therapy and of their ability to function well without it.

At the same time, our clients are wise in being concerned that if therapy ends too soon there will be a relapse or a return of the symptoms they had conquered and they will find themselves in another crisis point. As indicated by the answer to the victim question "What if it happens again?," families surviving trauma frequently emphasize that they do not want to return to the trauma-induced period of crisis. They wish to learn from their ordeal and become more resilient as a result.

This is quite normal. This phase of treatment must always address and develop a plan for relapse, because various life events such as anniversaries, family or developmental life cycle transitions, and other periods of high stress can be associated with triggered reactions. It is important to normalize this and anticipate how the family will cope effectively using their new skills. If the therapy is terminated appropriately, the family know that they can call on you again in time either as a therapist or as a temporary or part-time consultant. And they probably will.

## Prevention

At this phase of treatment we begin to emphasize prevention. A critical part of every survivor's healing theory is the part about lessons: what was learned from this experience, and how we can better prepare for future adversities. In the final phase this component can be emphasized even more.

Most families will be quite receptive to this prevention motive since they addressed the victim question: If something equally challenging happens in the future, will we cope better?

As the family enjoy a sense of accomplishment for working through the current crisis, the therapist should pose one or more crisis situations for the family's discussion. This allows them to apply the insights and skills developed in the intervention program and to be given the confidence that they will be able to face and overcome future adversities.

## Families as Survivors, Not Victims

As another method of reinforcing the intervention, the family could be asked to serve as a role model to other families seeking assistance. We often emphasize that they, by virtue of being exposed to such traumatic experiences and overcoming them, are now survivors rather than victims.

Some time ago, I (CRF) (Figley, 1985b) distinguished between a victim and a survivor, and we make the same distinctions for families at this phase of therapy. A victim is someone who is fearful of the future because of what happened to him or her. The victim is afraid of repeating the same pattern that will lead to another crisis and failure to cope. Survivors, on the other hand, focus on what they've accomplished by overcoming the trauma. Their achievements help them to feel resilient. As a result, they are even more confident in their ability to deal with future challenges. They can transform traumatic events that were at one time stumbling blocks into stepping stones to recovery and even thriving. This adversity-related growth has been part of human adaptation across gender, history, the life course of human development, and cultures worldwide (Figley, 2002a).

The process of recovering from traumatic events is the transformation from being a victim to being a survivor. Victims and survivors are similar in that they both experienced a traumatic event. But while the victim has been immobilized and discouraged by the event, the survivor has overcome the traumatic memories and become mobile. The survivor draws on the experiences of coping with the catastrophe as a source of strength, while the victim remains immobilized.

What separates victims from survivors is a conception about life, an attitude about the safety, joy, and mastery of being a human being. Being a survivor, then, is making peace with the memories of the catastrophe and its wake.

If the family agree to serve as survivor role models, they are told that they might be called on sometime in the near future to talk with another family who are in the process of recovering from a highly stressful event. The family could be reminded of their feelings of discouragement, shame, confusion, and hopelessness prior to treatment. Such a survivor role model family might have been quite useful to them at that point, giving them hope and reassurance.

## Summary and Conclusion

This final phase of the treatment program, then, involves bringing the intervention to a successful closure. Bringing closure is done first by ensuring that the family clients are aware of and celebrate the fact that they have reached their treatment objectives.

This final phase also involves ensuring that the client family are well prepared for future adversities. They need to feel confident in what actions they will take and equipped with sufficient resources and coping abilities and skills to ensure their success.

This phase for some families and some therapists is either the hardest or the easiest, because it involves saying good-bye. What is important is the effort of ensuring that the client families appreciate their accomplishments of successfully coping with an extraordinary traumatic stressor and that they are sufficiently equipped with the resources (skills and attitudes or values) necessary for coping with future potential traumas.

## The Murray Family

This final phase was quite a relief with the Murrays. Both children were getting bored in session and were excused except for the last session. It was clear that this phase of treatment was for them somewhat anticlimactic. They had successfully recapitulated the details of their current trauma and related ones of the past, had recognized and eliminated unwanted family relationship patterns that emerged to cope with the crisis, and had developed an effective healing theory that would sustain them through—and indeed help them prevent—future traumas.

During the final session the therapist asked Tammy and then the father to describe what the family would do to cope with the results if a fire destroyed their home, or if Mrs. Murray were hospitalized for several months, or if a pet died. Their responses were polite but matter of fact and somewhat patronizing, as if they were saying, "Poor old doctor just will not let us go until he is certain we are okay."

Toward the end of the final session, the therapist tried to develop a context for allowing them to return to therapy at any time without any sense of shame or defeat, while at the same time reinforcing that they were primarily responsible for effective adaptation and readjustment to their trauma.

> *Therapist:* As we agreed at the end of the last session, I would like to see you all back here for fifteen minutes in three months (no charge). It will be an opportunity to talk about things, face to face, and to answer any questions you might have. I want to emphasize now, and I will again in three months, that you all should feel good about yourselves as people and as a team, a family. I have tried to provide a place here to work on things, but you all did the work. I do hope that you will be willing to help other families when and if you can. You would be great survivor role models. And finally, don't be concerned if the trauma flares up again sometime in the future. It is natural to have bad memories or to get angry or confused about the past from time to time. It is an indication that you are sensitive and caring people. Any questions or comments? See you in three months.

Adversity stimulates growth under the right conditions. The Murray family grew. Facilitated by a professional qualified to work with traumatized families, they evolved in their brief therapy with new insight about their own behavior, thoughts, and emotions and those of other family members. Equally importantly, the family as a whole focused on surviving as a family, as a working team, and to getting back their life, though it is a "new normal"—a family changed forever but for the better, stronger and more resilient.

## Part three

# Empowering Family Trauma Therapists

# ten
# The Family Trauma Therapist

You are probably well aware at this point that the family trauma therapist faces some interesting and often daunting clinical challenges. For those of you who choose to help the family who have been traumatized, the challenges will be great, because working with families is much more encompassing than working with individuals. Couples and families have a remarkable ability to draw the therapist into their system, although most therapists resist this membership and attempt to remain unaligned, positioning themselves with various alliances for strategic reasons. However, the effort to remain unaligned takes enormous concentration. Moreover, the same kind of psychosocial mechanisms within families that make trauma "contagious," that create a context for family members to infect one another with their traumatic material, operate between clients who have been traumatized and the therapist. Remember, though, that the benefits can also be great.

This chapter describes some of the roles demonstrated by family trauma therapists: conveying a professional bearing and shifting between multiple roles to support the family's resilience. A later section of the chapter talks about the costs of caring: burnout, secondary traumatic stress reactions, injuries, and mental disorders from the work, and the obverse response: compassion satisfaction and growth from being a family trauma therapist.

# Clarifying the Therapist's Role

## Conveying Confidence

Wallace Denton refers to the wall in our offices with all our degrees, diplomas, and awards as our "credibility wall." Most often, he points out, the wall faces our clients. These credentials serve as important symbols for us and our clients. They suggest, in effect, "you are in good hands; I am an expert."

Ultimately, the key to successfully moving through the first phase of treatment is convincing the clients that you will be able to help them recover fully from the problems that brought them to therapy. Rapport with and reassurance from the therapist are certainly a very important part of building this professional confidence. Therapists should also attempt to convey that they are fully in charge, and that any extraordinary emotional session, setbacks in the recovery process, or other ordeals will be handled competently and efficiently. As a trauma therapist, the therapist should also convey a sense of emotional strength and security. The client family need to know that you can handle hearing their trauma story.

From the point of view of the clients, this sense of authority and confidence is often closely connected to the amount of experience of the therapist. You should not hesitate to weave into your interviews with the clients your many years of successful experience as a clinician, particularly one who has worked with families and individuals who have been traumatized. Seasoned therapists balance treating families as if they are unique with treating them consistently with the patterns seen in other families who have been traumatized, which, when recognized, can speed the treatment program.

But what if you are a new therapist or new to working with those who have experienced trauma or especially if you are a beginner trauma therapist working with families? You must recognize that this is a major challenge that will require not only additional study in the literature, but also additional time to bond with the family. Moreover, it is essential to work with a supervisor or, preferably, with a treatment team who may be working with individual family members, such as a marital therapist or a child therapist. Gradually, the family will embrace you as a useful resource.

## Shifting Roles

One of the challenges of doing family trauma treatment is dealing with the complexity of the multiple relationships involved. We have emphasized throughout this book that the impact of trauma is relational. This means that the family trauma therapist must be diligent about negotiating relationships with each family member, with family subsystems, and with the family as a whole using a trauma-informed approach. It means that, in addition to the usual roles that a family therapist takes, the family trauma therapist will take on a few roles specific to helping the family adapt in healthy ways.

Helping families who have been traumatized means being flexible regarding one's role as a family trauma therapist. Sometimes we need to be coaches. Sometimes we need to be teachers. Sometimes we need to be both counselors and just sounding boards. Sometimes we take one-down positions, yielding to the family's perspective, to provide more latitude and leverage with client families. Sometimes we must use less direct approaches, such as solution-focused therapy methods, or apply a strategy for changing behavior that was unwanted and unusual. Sometimes we need to be experts and serve as teachers and, at other times, we need to be learners while the family serves as the expert. Sometimes we need to be conductors orchestrating the family's interactions and, at other times, we need to be the audience, good listeners and keen observers of the family's interactions.

Along these same lines, at times we therapists need to be the power and authority within the system while at other times we need to be power brokers, skillfully helping families negotiate the power dynamics within the family system. As brokers, we work to ensure that all voices are heard while supporting the appropriate role of the adult caregivers as "in charge" of their family. And at times we need to be pressure gauges measuring the intensity of emotion in the family and helping the family regulate it by turning up or down the heat. At the same time we need to regulate our own emotions, knowing how much of our feelings to share with the family.

## Therapist Burden and Growth

As families are transformed as a result of adversity, so are therapists. Hearing family stories is often a wonderful treat for family therapists as they get to know their client families. When families share their trauma stories, however, the therapist also shares the pain and suffering. We often take these stories with us, creating last memories often accompanied by some intense emotions.

We have both discussed elsewhere the costs of caring as trauma therapists and have both experienced these costs in different ways and with different consequences (see Figley, 1995, 2002a). Compassion fatigue and secondary trauma were first identified in families who live with family members who have been traumatized by Zahave Solomon, who was studying the wives of soldiers with combat stress reactions (Z. Solomon, Mikulincer, Fried, & Wosner, 1987). The secondary traumatic stress reactions of trauma therapists are well known and were first discussed as burnout or burden of care (Figley & Kleber, 1995; Maslach & Leiter, 1997).

Sadly, we have seen some colleagues and friends abandon clinical work because of their inability to cope with the troubles of others. This is particularly true for those who work with "victims" of various catastrophes. Those therapists most at risk of abandoning their proper role, however, are those who begin to view themselves as saviors, or at least as rescuers. Some of these clinical "rescuers" do not have the resources and skills to avoid having this role intrude in their life, becoming addicted or at least succumbing to countertransference. These can be particularly problematical in working with families.

NiCarthy, Merriam, and Coffman (1984) urged those who work with abused women, for example, to become familiar with the stages and signs of burnout in working with this population. The same kinds of warnings can be applied to working with other types of traumatized populations. Among the symptoms they cite are emotional and physical exhaustion that includes but is not limited to headaches, muscle tension, depression, boredom, apathy, absenteeism, decline in performance, hypertension, insomnia, irritability, increased anxiety, increased smoking, drinking, drug dependency, other addictions, dysfunctional escape activities (overeating, daydreaming), stress-related physical and emotional ailments, tension with family and/or friends, self-doubt and blame, and general disillusionment.

The emergence in the 1990s of terms and theories about work-related problems of those who work with the traumatized started with the publication in 1995 of *Compassion Fatigue: Theory, Research, and Treatment* (Figley, 1995), followed a few years later with *Treating Compassion Fatigue* (Figley, 2002b). Today there are more than two dozen books on such topics. Collectively they offer excellent tools (e.g., the ProQual by Stamm, 2006; the Secondary Traumatic Stress Scale (Bride, Robinson, Yegidis, & Figley, 2004), and the Boscarino Brief CF Scale (Boscarino, Figley, & Adams, 2004).

## Help for the Helpers

There are ways of overcoming these problems. Among the many methods of both avoiding and eliminating the "savior syndrome," NiCarthy et al. (1984) and others (Cherniss, 1980; Edelwich & Brodsky, 1980; Figley, 1982, 1985b; Maslach, 1982; Pines, Aronson, & Kafray, 1981; Rando, 1984) suggest the following:

1   **Comprehensive education about stress and coping.** Figley has urged for many years (see, for example, Figley & McCubbin, 1983) that professional training in the helping professions should generally include courses and in-service training programs that focus on normative and catastrophic stressors. These programs should identify not only the common methods that individuals, families, and other systems use in reaction to stress but also

the stressors that are unique to the helping professions, particularly the pitfalls in working with traumatized clients.

2  **Developing and maintaining membership in supportive networks.** Therapists often cannot help but bring home their work. This is particularly true if the thoughts and feelings associated with clients involuntarily intrude on their personal life. Often it requires another professional who has experienced these intrusions to truly understand and provide emotional support. It is appropriate, therefore, to reserve sufficient time at the end of a case conference or professional meeting for some personal processing. It would be an opportunity to share the emotional burdens of clinical work without shame or indignity. Group members can provide emotional support and encouragement, ingredients that are vital to the maintenance of good mental health. They can also serve as role models and sources of information and ideas about methods of coping.

3  **Focus on the joylessness of the lives of our clients.** Some of us may even feel guilty for feeling contentment and satisfaction with ourselves and our families. Yet our own life satisfaction makes us more adept at helping others find such satisfaction. Cultivating interesting hobbies, enjoying vacations and recreational activities, and spending time with family and friends are good not only for us but also for our clients.

4  **Setting realistic goals, limits, and boundaries.** Finally, we have learned over the years that we have just so much time, energy, interest, and sensitivity. We have learned to distribute these finite resources according to our values and to be constantly vigilant about over-distribution. Otherwise, we have an insufficient amount of time, energy, interest, and sensitivity for our family, friends, and ourselves. As professionals, we have suffered a great deal at times when we were not vigilant enough and sacrificed these personal resources for other things (such as career and clients). Our worst experiences with clients—traumatized or not—were with those who wanted more than we could give. Our salvation was the realization that we had done as much as we could at the time and that we could help the client and another helper begin where we left off.

## The Transformative Work of Helping Traumatized Families

We entered the fields of family therapy and traumatic stress many years ago (1974 and 1981). We have never regretted it. We believe that this is true for a majority of our colleagues who have treated families. There were few guidelines for working with families who had been traumatized at that time. What kept us all focused and resilient as practitioners, though working with the traumatized, was the personal and professional satisfaction of knowing that we had made a significant contribution to the recovery of individuals and families struggling to overcome hardship.

Moreover, according to some theories of therapists' adversities, what can lead to compassion fatigue can also lead to compassion growth; the experience of distress associated with treating the traumatized, including family therapists, can lead to vicarious resilience (Hernandez et al., 2007). One of the reasons why therapists experience personal and professional growth is having the opportunity to work with families who have lived through incredible adversity and who have survived. Hearing from and observing these amazing survivors is a humbling yet growth-producing experience.

Another reason is associated with compassion satisfaction (Stamm, 1995) for the work: a considerable number of practitioners recognize that what they do is transformative. We have experienced tremendous emotional satisfaction from our professional work in the fields of family therapy and traumatic stress. We can recall professional achievements, such as completing a first book, *Stress Disorders Among Vietnam Veterans: Theory, Research, and Treatment* (Figley, 1978) (CRF) or finishing the manual for Strengthening Family Coping Resources and having it implemented successfully in clinics (LJK). We felt an extraordinary sense of pride and relief. The relief came from believing that we had made a contribution, not just to the mental health field but also to helping a group of men and women, children, and families who were not as lucky as we are and whom we wished very much to help.

## Conclusion

We called this chapter "The Family Trauma Therapist" for a reason. The concept of therapist is rooted in the concept of healer. The meaning of "healer" is literally "remover of arrows." Therapists, in contrast to those who enable patients to manage the arrow, go beyond holding hands and giving reassurance or, worse, being expected to fix the problem not just the symptoms.

We tried throughout this chapter to discuss the role of the client family's arrows remover. There are some relevant points.

First, it takes skills to remain neutral when working with couples and families in times of crisis, such as in the wake of a traumatic event. As a result, those new to working with systems or the traumatized need to prepare for the learning curve: the slope over time of understanding and skill required of an effective family trauma therapist. Second, family trauma therapists play many roles that collectively represent a highly valued resource for the client family struggling with a crisis caused by a sudden, unexpected catastrophe. Third, there is a cost to caring that requires attention to boundaries, stress management, and absorbing the good with the bad. We touched on these matters rather briefly.

We believe that if you are a family seeking a therapist to help remove the trauma-associated pain permanently you should expect no less than what we have described here. If you are a family therapist we urge you to consider the remarkable impact of trauma on families: trauma may dramatically change how families respond to adversity; the impact is systemic, affecting nearly all aspects of family life; and family traumas can have an extraordinary impact that reverberates throughout the family system, changing and straining family relationships, which in turn reverberates through outside relationships.

The final point here is associated with the costs of caring, which were discussed briefly in the chapter. Charles Figley's (1995) book on compassion fatigue was published six years after the first edition of the book you are reading, which itself was first applied to nurses in 1992 (Joinson). Since this time most students who go into trauma work have been well aware of the toxic nature of listening to others' troubles all day, especially the traumatized. We hope that this updated version will emphasize the importance of self-care and a significant effort on the part of clients, employers, and insurance companies to appreciate how the work of healer drains the practitioner.

The following chapter continues the discussion of the challenges of trauma work, with special consideration for the traumatized families requiring help.

# eleven

# **Epilogue**

## Implications for Practice, Policy, and Research

As therapists struggle to bring closure to a clinical case, authors struggle to bring closure to a book, particularly clinical authors. But just as the antidote for the former is to rely on one's objectives as an indicator of completion, so too must the objectives of a book, this book, provide direction for closure, an ending. We will first discuss the objectives with which we began this book and then turn to the implications of this work, as we see them today.

Approaches to helping families who have been traumatized emerge from a wide variety of scientific inquiries about families who do not ordinarily seek treatment. Indeed, the clinical literature, by focusing on psychopathology and dysfunction, frequently represents families—either implicitly or explicitly—as the cause of mental illness. We, however, challenge this view and suggest that families, in particular, and social support networks and groups, in general, provide a vital and often overlooked function in fostering mental health and well-being (see Pilisuk & Parks, 1986).

Our approach to helping families impacted by trauma assumes that the family was functioning acceptably well for all its members prior to the impact of the traumatic event. Moreover, victimized family members may find more effective emotional support from sources other than the family. Even well-intentioned families can be enormously ineffective in helping some family members, for a variety of reasons. But in spite of these obvious limitations of utilizing or empowering families to help each other, we believe it is the most successful path for most. By intervening at the family systems level, we believe that not only will the pain and suffering of members be alleviated but also, as a result of the intervention, the family will be more equipped to cope effectively with future challenges.

From the beginning we have tried to share with you the theories, perspectives, basic assumptions, and methods we use for helping families who have been traumatized. Specifically, we wanted to reach at least three separate objectives:

1  to review what we know about families who have experienced trauma, including definitions of some important concepts and several theoretical models that clarify these concepts;
2  to discuss the typical ways families cope with trauma, by presenting a model of family adaptation to trauma; and
3  to describe a comprehensive approach to treating a variety of families suffering from the aftershocks of their trauma.

We tried to focus the first part of the book on the first objective. In the first chapter, we noted how and why we view families as systems. Also in the first chapter, we defined what we meant by trauma and how we conceptualize families who have been traumatized.

The third chapter included most of the material for addressing the second objective of the book. In the second chapter, we also reviewed the ways families are naturally supportive of one another. Indeed, they are so effective and efficient in helping family members distressed by their experiences of trauma (detecting traumatic stress, urging confrontation of the stressor, urging recapitulation of the catastrophe, and facilitating resolution of the conflicts) that we have tailored our empowerment treatment approach based on these naturally existing methods.

A way of summarizing the powerful role families play in human functioning and the process by which the family systems confront and recover from trauma is the Family Trauma Adaptation Model presented in Chapter three. It provided a context for appreciating the variety of ways families cope with a wide variety of stressors and clarified the characteristics that tend to differentiate functional and dysfunctional family coping, which were described at the end of the chapter.

Part two addressed the third objective of the book. Chapter four presented the theoretical building blocks for our approach to conceptualizing, assessing, and treating families impacted by trauma. Here we noted that we attempt to empower the family to make peace with the past and take charge of their lives, and that this kind of intervention could be categorized as primary prevention, as well as secondary prevention. In addition to helping families make peace with the past, we try to educate them about trauma, traumatic stress, family functioning, and healing. Moreover, we attempt to enhance their natural resources, including their basic family supportiveness and collaborative coping skills. Beginning with Chapter five, the chapters included a detailed description of our five-phase empowering approach to helping families who have been traumatized, including a detailed description of the treatment preconditions, methods of assessment, and intervention strategies.

## Challenges for Practice and Research

It should be obvious at this point that families are not only complex, but also extraordinarily important to human survival, resilience, and thriving. The family is both a source of support and a context for recovery but can often also be a maintainer of symptoms, a caustic container, and traumatogenic. This dichotomy has implications for both practice and research.

Moreover, there is often an intergenerational nature to family trauma: trauma history is passed down without consciousness-cycles of intrafamilial trauma followed by family member acceptance. As a result of this long-term adaptation process, the effects of any one trauma may be difficult to isolate, and patterns of behavior or coping may be confusing in the here and now.

This is especially challenging for the therapist working with families that include one or more members who are, themselves, family trauma perpetrators.

Obviously, our approach to helping traumatized families is based on numerous assumptions that need to be tested and verified or changed. The major assumption of this approach to family trauma therapy, for example, is that treatment should, at the very least, focus on the healing resources of the family system and attempt to restore them at least to pre-trauma levels. This assumption should of course be tested under rigorous scientific conditions in order to be supported or refuted.

Our family empowerment approach certainly should be tested and contrasted with others that also purport to be effective in helping families adapt to trauma. Assuming that this approach is useful and appropriate, what are the implications for future research and treatment innovation? Certainly, traumatic events and the associated stress of individuals and social systems have always existed. Most recently, traumatic stress studies have made significant strides in identifying the major parameters that account for why people are traumatized and the process by which they recover. Moreover, the social support systems and the family in particular are extremely important resources in the recovery process. Comprehensive and effective intervention programs to prevent and treat traumatic stress must include some form of family treatment.

Beyond outcome studies, however, it is important to verify the findings of Kishur (1984), who found evidence of the chiasmal effect of the "transfer" of traumatic symptoms to supporters. It is important to include this in future studies of the incidence and prevalence of PTSD among various groups of victims and evaluation of the victims' closest supporters.

Beyond our approach and model for treating traumatized families is the reality that families are difficult to study because families are among the most complex of living systems. Equally important are the research challenges: Studying systems is messy and requires sophisticated models, designs, and methods.

## Conclusion

As we have tried to demonstrate throughout this book, the effective and efficient treatment of families who have experienced trauma requires careful attention to many factors. One of the most important factors is the client's access to an effective social support system (Burge & Figley, 1987). For example, victims who are separated from family and friends and lack the social skills to establish and maintain close interpersonal relationships are more vulnerable to traumatic stress. In contrast, those who enjoy an active and vibrant social life are able to avoid and quickly overcome troubling life events. For those clients who do have access to social support, particularly intact systems such as a family, the system itself may provide the most powerful healing resource. Because the family has such a central role in helping its members cope with trauma, it is the natural unit of intervention in helping those members. Although few have discussed the utility of family therapy in traumatic stress treatment, we hope that this book has illustrated the role of family therapy in treating not only the victims but also the co-victims, fellow family members, and the family system within which they reside. By selecting the family as the unit of intervention, we are assured not only of ameliorating the unwanted side effects of traumatic stress but also of equipping the family to cope more effectively with any future adversities.

# References

Abidin, R. R. (1990). *The Parenting Stress Index Short Form: Test manual.* Charlottesville, VA: Pediatric Psychology Press.

Achenbach, T. M., & Edelbrock, C. (1991). *Manual for the Child Behavior Checklist.* Burlington, VT: University of Vermont Department of Psychiatry.

American Psychiatric Association. (1994). *Diagnostic and statistical manual of mental disorders* (4th ed.). Washington, DC: Author.

American Psychiatric Association. (2004). *Practice guideline for the treatment of patients with acute stress disorder and posttraumatic stress disorder.* Arlington, VA: Author.

Angell, G. B., Dennis, B. G., & Dumain, L. E. (1998). Spirituality, resilience, and narrative: Coping with parental death. *Families in Society, 79*(6), 615–630.

Appleyard, K., & Osofsky, J. D. (2003). Parenting after trauma: Supporting parents and caregivers in the treatment of children impacted by violence. *Infant Mental Health Journal, 24*(2), 111–125.

Bandura, A. (1989). Regulation of cognitive processes through perceived self-efficacy. *Developmental Psychology, 25*, 729–735.

Berg, C. A., Meegan, S. P., & Deviney, F. P. (1998). A social-contextual model of coping with everyday problems across the lifespan. *International Journal of Behavioral Development, 22*(2), 239–261.

Bernstein, D. P., & Fink, L. (1998). *Child Trauma Questionnaire manual.* San Antonio, TX: The Psychological Corporation.

Besley, A. C. (2002). Foucault and the turn to narrative therapy. *British Journal of Guidance and Counselling, 30*(2), 125–143.

Bishop, D. S., Epstein, N. B., & Baldwin, L. M. (1980). Structuring a family assessment interview. *Canadian Family Physician, 26*(November), 1534–1537.

Blake, D. D., Weathers, F. W., Nagy, L. M., Kaloupek, D. G., Gusman, F. D., Charney, D. S., et al. (1995). The development of a clinician-administered PTSD scale. *Journal of Traumatic Stress, 8*, 75–90.

Bohanek, J. G., Marin, K. A., Fivush, R., & Duke, M. (2006). Family narrative interaction and children's sense of self. *Family Process, 45*(1), 39–54.

Boscarino, J. A., Figley, C. R., & Adams, R. E. (2004). Evidence of compassion fatigue following the September 11 terrorist attacks: A study of secondary trauma among social workers in New York. *International Journal of Emergency Mental Health, 6*(2), 98–108.

Bowlby, J. (1961). Processes of mourning. *International Journal of Psychoanalysis, 44*, 317.

Bowlby, J. (1969). *Attachment and loss: Vol. 1*. New York: Basic Books.

Bowlby, J. (1980). *Attachment and loss: Vol. 3. Loss, sadness, and depression*. New York: Basic Books.

Breslau, N., Chilcoat, H. D., Kessler, R. C., & Davis, G. C. (1999). Previous exposure to trauma and PTSD effects of subsequent trauma: Results from the Detroit Area Survey of Trauma. *American Journal of Psychiatry, 156*, 902–907.

Bride, B. E., Robinson, M. M., Yegidis, B., & Figley, C. R. (2004). Development and validation of the Secondary Traumatic Stress Scale. *Research on Social Work Practice, 14*(1), 27–36.

Briere, J. (1996). *Manual for the Trauma Symptom Checklist for Children (TSCC)*. Lutz, FL: Psychological Assessment Resources.

Bronfenbrenner, U. (1979). *The ecology of human development*. Cambridge, MA: Harvard University Press.

Brownell, A., & Shumaker, S. A. (1984). Social support: An introduction to a complex phenomenon. *Journal of Social Issues, 4*, 1–9.

Burge, S. K., & Figley, C. R. (1987). The social support scale: Development and initial estimates of reliability and validity. *Victimology, 12*(1), 14–22.

Burgess, A. W., & Holmstron, L. L. (1979). *Rape: Crisis and recovery*. Bowie, MD: Brady.

Busby, D. M., Crane, D. R., Larson, J. H., & Christensen, C. (1995). A revision of the Dyadic Adjustment Scale for use with distressed and nondistressed couples: Construct hierarchy and multidimensional scales. *Journal of Marital and Family Therapy, 21*(3), 289–308.

Cahill, S. P., & Foa, E. B. (2007). Psychological theories of PTSD. In M. J. Friedman, T. M. Keane, & P. A. Resick (Eds.), *Handbook of PTSD: Science and practice* (pp. 55–77). New York: Guilford Press.

Cannon, W. B. (1939). *The wisdom of the body*. New York: Morton.

Caplan, G. (1964). *Principles of preventive psychiatry*. New York: Basic Books.

Carr, A. (2000). Evidence-based practice in family therapy and systemic consultation. *Journal of Family Therapy, 22*(1), 29–60.

Carver, C. S. (1998). Resilience and thriving: Issues, models, and linkages. *Journal of Social Issues, 54*, 245–266.

Catalano, S. (2007). *Intimate partner violence in the United States*. Washington, DC: US Department of Justice, Office of Justice Programs, Bureau of Justice Statistics.

Ceballo, R., & McLoyd, V. C. (2002). Social support and parenting in poor, dangerous neighborhoods. *Child Development, 73*(4), 1310–1321.

Cherniss, C. (1980). *Staff burnout: Job stress in the human services*. Newbury Park, CA: Sage.

Cicchetti, D., Cummings, E. M., Greenberg, M. T., & Marvin, R. (1990). An organizational perspective on attachment beyond infancy: Implications for theory, measurement, and research. In M. T. Greenberg, D. Cicchetti, & E. M. Cummings (Eds.), *Attachment in the preschool years: Theory, research, and intervention* (pp. 3–49). Chicago: University of Chicago Press.

Cloitre, M., Koenen, K. C., Cohen, L. R., & Han, H. (2002). Skills training in affective and interpersonal regulation followed by exposure: A phase-based treatment for PTSD related to childhood abuse. *Journal of Consulting and Clinical Psychology, 70*(5), 1067–1074.

Cohen, J. A., Bukstein, O., Walter, H., Benson, R. S., Christman, A., Farchione, T. R., et al. (2010). Practice parameter for the assessment and treatment of children and adolescents with posttraumatic stress disorder. *Journal of the American Academy of Child and Adolescent Psychiatry, 49*(4), 414–430.

Collins, K., Connors, K., Donohue, A., Gardner, S., Goldblatt, E., Hayward, A., et al. (2010). *Understanding the impact of trauma and urban poverty on family systems: Risks, resilience, and interventions.* Baltimore: Family Informed Trauma Treatment Center. Retrieved August 9, 2012, from http://fittcenter.umaryland.edu/White Paper.aspx

Compas, B. E., Connor-Smith, J. K., Saltzman, H., Thomsen, A. H., & Wadsworth, M. E. (2001). Coping with stress during childhood and adolescence: Problems, progress, and potential in theory and research. *Psychological Bulletin, 127*(1), 87–127.

Conger, R. D., Wallace, L. E., Sun, Y., Simons, R. L., McLoyd, V. C., & Brody, G. H. (2002). Economic pressure in African American families: A replication and extension of the family stress model. *Developmental Psychology, 38*(2), 179–193.

Cook, A., Spinazzola, J., Ford, J., Lanktree, C., Blaustein, M., Cloitre, M., et al. (2005). Complex trauma in children and adolescents. *Psychiatric Annals, 35*(5), 390–398.

Delage, M. (2002). Strengthening family resilience in traumatic situations. *Therapie Familiale, 23*, 269–287.

Derogatis, L. R. (1993). *Brief Symptom Inventory (BSI).* Minneapolis, MN: National Computer Systems.

Derogatis, L. R. and P. M. Spencer. (1982). *The Brief Symptom Inventory (BSI) administration, scoring, and procedures manual.* Baltimore: Johns Hopkins University School of Medicine, Clinical Psychometrics Research Unit.

Donnelly, C. L., & Amaya-Jackson, L. (2002). Post-traumatic stress disorder in children and adolescents: Epidemiology, diagnosis and treatment options. *Paediatric Drugs, 4*(3), 159–170.

Edelwich, J., & Brodsky, A. (1980). *Burn-out: Stages of disillusionment in the helping professions.* New York: Human Sciences Press.

Ehde, D.M., Patterson, D.R., Wiechman, S.A., & Wilson, L.G. (2000). Post-traumatic stress symptoms and distress 1 year after burn injury. *Journal of Burn Care and Rehabilitation, 21*, 105–111.

Eitinger, L. (1982). The effects of captivity. In F. M. Ochberg & D. A. Soskis (Eds.), *Victims of terrorism* (pp. 73–94). Boulder, CO: Westview.

Epstein, N. B., Baldwin, L. M., & Bishop, D. S. (1983). The McMaster Family Assessment Device. *Journal of Marital and Family Therapy, 9*, 171–180.

Felitti, V. J., & Anda, R. F. (2009). The relationship of adverse childhood experiences to adult medical disease, psychiatric disorders, and sexual behavior: Implications for healthcare. In R. Lanius & E. Vermetten (Eds.), *The hidden epidemic: The impact of early life trauma on health and disease.* Cambridge: Cambridge University Press.

Felson, R., & Outlaw, M. (2007). The control motive and marital violence. *Violence and Victims, 22*(4), 387–407.

Fiese, B. H. (2006). *Family routines and rituals.* New Haven, CT: Yale University Press.

Fiese, B., & Wamboldt, F. (2000). Family routines, rituals, and asthma management: A proposal for family-based strategies to increase treatment adherence. *Families, Systems and Health, 18*(4), 405–418.

Figley, C. R. (1973). Child density and the marital relationship. *Journal of Marriage and the Family, 45*(3), 211–223.

Figley, C. R. (1978). Psychosocial adjustment among Vietnam veterans: An overview of the research. In C. R. Figley (Ed.), *Stress disorders among Vietnam veterans: Theory, research, and treatment* (pp. 57–70). New York: Brunner/Mazel.

Figley, C. R. (1979). *Combat as disaster: Treating combat veterans as survivors.* Invited address to the American Psychiatric Association, Chicago.

Figley, C. R. (1980). *The algorithmic approach to treating post-traumatic stress reactions.* Presented at a clinical workshop on treating combat-related stress disorders, Veterans Administration Regional Medical Education Center, St. Louis, MO.

Figley, C. R. (1982). *Traumatization and comfort: Close relationships may be hazardous to your health.* Invited lecture, Texas Tech University, Lubbock, TX.

Figley, C. R. (1983). Catastrophes: An overview of family reactions. In C. R. Figley & H. I. McCubbin (Eds.), *Stress and the family: Vol. 2. Coping with catastrophe* (pp. 3–20). New York: Brunner/Mazel.

Figley, C. R. (1985a). The family as victim: Mental health implications. *Psychiatry, 6,* 283–291.

Figley, C. R. (1985b). From victim to survivor: Social responsibility in the wake of catastrophe. In C. R. Figley (Ed.), *Trauma and its wake: The study and treatment of post-traumatic stress disorder* (pp. 398–416). New York: Brunner/Mazel.

Figley, C. R. (1985c). Introduction. In C. R. Figley (Ed.), *Trauma and its wake: The study and treatment of post-traumatic stress disorder* (pp. xvii–xxvi). New York: Brunner/Mazel.

Figley, C. R. (1986). Traumatic stress: The role of the family and social support systems. In C. R. Figley (Ed.), *Trauma and its wake: Vol. 2. Post-traumatic stress disorder: Theory, research, and treatment* (pp. 39–56). New York: Brunner/Mazel.

Figley, C. R. (1988a). The "field" of traumatic stress. *Journal of Traumatic Stress, 1*(1), 1–14.

Figley, C. R. (1988b). A five-phase treatment of PTSD in families. *Journal of Traumatic Stress, 1*(1), 126–141.

Figley, C. R. (1988c). Post-traumatic family therapy. In F. M. Ochberg (Ed.), *Post-traumatic therapy and victims of violence* (pp. 83–109). New York: Brunner/Mazel.

Figley, C. R. (Ed.). (1995). *Compassion fatigue: Secondary traumatic stress disorders from treating the traumatized.* New York: Brunner/Mazel.

Figley, C. R. (Ed.). (1998). *Burnout in families: The systemic costs of caring.* Boca Raton, FL: CRC Press.

Figley, C. R. (Ed.). (2002a). *Brief treatments for the traumatized: A project of the Green Cross Foundation.* Westport, CT: Greenwood.

Figley, C. R. (Ed.). (2002b). *Treating compassion fatigue.* New York: Routledge.

Figley, C. R., & Kleber, R. J. (1995). Beyond the "victim": Secondary traumatic stress. In R. J. Kleber, C. R. Figley, & B. Gersons (Eds.), *Beyond trauma: Cultural and societal dynamics.* New York: Plenum.

Figley, C. R., & McCubbin, H. I. (1983). Looking to the future: Research, education, treatment, and policy. In C. R. Figley & H. I. McCubbin (Eds.), *Stress and the family: Vol. 2. Coping with catastrophe* (pp. 185–196). New York: Brunner/Mazel.

Figley, C. R., & Nash, W. P. (Eds.). (2007). *Combat stress injury: Theory, research, and management.* New York: Routledge.

Finkelhor, D., Ormrod, R., Turner, H. J., & Hamby, S. L. (2005). The victimization of children and youth: A comprehensive national survey. *Child Maltreatment, 10*(1), 5–25.

Fisch, R., Weakland, J. H., & Segal, L. (1982). *The tactics of change: Doing therapy briefly.* San Francisco: Jossey-Bass.

Foa, E. B., Keane, T. M., Friedman, M. J., & Cohen, J. A. (Eds.). (2008). *Effective treatments for PTSD: Practice guidelines from the International Society for Traumatic Stress Studies* (2nd ed.). New York: Guilford Press.

Folkman, S., & Moskowitz, J. T. (2000). Positive affect and the other side of coping. *American Psychologist, 55*(6), 647–654.

Forbes, D., Creamer, M., Bisson, J. I., Cohen, J. A., Crow, B. E., Foa, E.B., et al. (2010). A guide to guidelines for the treatment of PTSD and related conditions. *Journal of Traumatic Stress, 23*(5), 537–552.

Fraser, J. S. (1989). The strategic rapid intervention approach. In C. R. Figley (Ed.), *Treating stress in families* (pp. 122–157). New York: Brunner/Mazel.

Freedman, J., & Combs, G. (1996). *Narrative therapy: The social construction of preferred realities.* New York: Norton.

Friedman, M. J., Resick, P. A., & Keane, T. M. (2007). PTSD: Twenty-five years of progress and challenges. In M. J. Friedman, T. M. Keane, & P. A. Resick (Eds.), *Handbook of PTSD: Science and practice* (pp. 3–18). New York: Guilford Press.

Gagne, M., & Bouchard, C. (2004). Family dynamics associated with the use of psychologically violent parental practices. *Journal of Family Violence, 19*(2), 117–130.

Gelles, R. J., & Maynard, P. E. (1987). A structural family systems approach to intervention in cases of family violence. *Family Relations, 38*, 270–275.

Ghosh-Ippen, C., Ford, J., Racusin, R., Acker, M., Bosquet, K., Rogers, C., et al. (2002). *Trauma Events Screening Inventory-Parent Report revised.* San Francisco: Child Trauma Research Project of the Early Trauma Network and National Center for PTSD Dartmouth Child Trauma Research Group.

Gibaud-Wallston, J., & Wandersman, L. P. (1978). *Development and utility of the Parenting Sense of Competence Scale.* Paper presented at the 86th Annual Convention of the American Psychological Association, Toronto, Ontario, Canada.

Gleser, G., Green, B. L., & Winget, C. (1981). *Prolonged psychosocial effects of disaster: A study of Buffalo Creek.* New York: Academic Press.

Gottlieb, B. H. (Ed.). (1983). *Social support strategies: Guidelines for mental health practice.* Newbury Park, CA: Sage.

Gottlieb, B. H. (Ed.). (1988). *Marshaling social support: Formats, processes, and effects.* Newbury Park, CA: Sage.

Green, B. L., Wilson, J. P., & Lindy, J. (1985). Conceptualizing post-traumatic stress disorder: A psychosocial framework. In C. R. Figley (Ed.), *Trauma and its wake: The study and treatment of post-traumatic stress disorder* (pp. 53–72). New York: Brunner/Mazel.

Griffin, S. (1991). The way we stand. In E. Roberts & E. Amidon (Eds.), *Earth prayers from around the world: 365 prayers, poems, and invocations for honoring the Earth.* New York: HarperCollins.

Guerney, B. G. (1977). *Relationship enhancement: Skill-training programs for therapy, problem prevention, and enrichment.* San Francisco: Jossey-Bass.

Guerney, B. G. (1982). Relationship enhancement. In E. K. Marshall & P. D. Kurtz (Eds.), *Interpersonal helping skills* (pp. 482–518). San Francisco: Jossey-Bass.

Haden, C. A. (1998). Reminiscing with different children: Relating maternal stylistic consistency and sibling similarity in talk about the past. *Developmental Psychology, 34*(1), 99–114.

Haley, J. (1973). *Uncommon therapy.* New York: Norton.

Haley, J. (1976). *Problem-solving therapy.* San Francisco: Jossey-Bass.

Haley, J. (1984). *Ordeal therapy: Unusual ways to change behavior.* San Francisco: Jossey-Bass.

Harris, C. J. (1991). A family crisis-intervention model for the treatment of post-traumatic stress reaction. *Journal of Traumatic Stress, 4*(2), 195–207.

Harvey, J. H., & Pauwels, B. G. (2000). *Post-traumatic stress theory: Research and application.* Philadelphia: Brunner/Mazel.

Harvey, M. R., & Herman, J. L. (1994). Amnesia, partial amnesia, and delayed recall among adult survivors of childhood trauma. *Consciousness and Cognition, 3*, 295–306.

Herman, J. L. (1986). History of violence in an outpatient population. *American Journal of Orthopsychiatry, 567*, 137–141.

Hernandez, P., Gangsei, D., & Engstrom, D. (2007). Vicarious resilience: A new concept in work with those who survive trauma. *Family Process, 46*, 229–241.

Hester, R. L. (2004). Early memory and narrative therapy. *Journal of Individual Psychology, 60*(4), 338–347.

Hetherington, E. M., Cox, M., and Cox, R. (1976). Divorced fathers. *The Family Coordinator, 25*, 417–428.

Hill, J., Fonagy, P., Safier, E., & Sargent, J. (2003). The ecology of attachment in the family. *Family Process, 42*, 205–221.

Hill, R. (1949). *Families under stress.* New York: Harper & Row.

Hill, R., & Hansen, D. (1965). The family in disaster. In G. Baker & D. S. Chapman (Eds.), *Man and society in disaster* (pp. 37–51). New York: Basic Books.

Hobfoll, S. E. (1988). *The ecology of stress.* Washington, DC: Hemisphere.

Hobfoll, S. E. (1989). Conservation of resources: A new attempt at conceptualizing stress. *American Psychologist, 44*(3), 513–524.

Hobfoll, S. E., Johnson, R. J., Ennis, N., & Jackson, A. P. (2003). Resource loss, resource gain, and emotional outcomes among inner city women. *Journal of Personality and Social Psychology, 84*, 632–643.

Hobfoll, S. E., & Lilly, R. S. (1993). Resource conservation as a strategy for community psychology. *Journal of Community Psychology, 21*, 128–148.

Hobfoll, S. E., Lilly, R. S., & Jackson, A. P. (1992). Conservation of social resources and the self. In H. O. F. Veiel & U. Baumann (Eds.), *The meaning and measurement of social support* (pp. 125–141). Washington, DC: Hemisphere.

Holahan, C. J., Moos, R. H., & Bonin, L. A. (1997). Social support, coping, and psychological adjustment: A resources model. In G. Pierce, B. Lakey, I. Sarason, &

B. Sarason (Eds.), *Sourcebook of theory and research on social support and personality* (pp. 169–186). New York: Plenum.

Horowitz, M. J. (1986). *Stress response syndromes* (2nd ed.). Northvale, NJ: Jason Aronson.

Howes, P. W., Cicchetti, D., Toth, S. L., & Rogosch, F. A. (2000). Affective, organizational, and relational characteristics of maltreating families: A systems perspective. *Journal of Family Psychology, 14,* 95–110.

Hunsley, J., Best, M., Lefebvre, M., & Vito, D. (2001). The seven item short form of the Dyadic Adjustment Scale: Further evidence for the construct validity. *American Journal of Family Therapy, 29*(4), 325–335.

Jacobson, G., Strickler, M., & Morley, W. (1968). Generic and individual approaches to crisis intervention. *American Journal of Public Health, 58,* 338–343.

Johnson, D. M., Palmieri, P. A., Jackson, A. P., & Hobfoll, S. E. (2007). Emotional numbing weakens abused inner-city women's resiliency resources. *Journal of Traumatic Stress, 20,* 197–206.

Joinson, C. (1992). Coping with compassion fatigue. *Nursing, 22*(4), 116–122.

Kazak, A. E. (1989). Families of chronically ill children: A systems and social-ecological model of adaptation and challenge. *Journal of Consulting and Clinical Psychology, 57,* 25–30.

Kazdin, A. E., & Wilcoxin, L. A. (1976). Systemic desensitization and nonspecific treatment effects: A methodological evaluation. *Psychological Bulletin, 83,* 729–758.

Kessler, R. C., Sonnega, A., Bromet, E., Hughes, M., & Nelson, C. B. (1995). Posttraumatic stress disorder in the National Comorbidity Survey. *Archives of General Psychiatry, 52*(12), 1048–1060.

Kiser, L. J. (2007). Protecting children from the dangers of urban poverty. *Clinical Psychology Review, 27,* 211–225.

Kiser, L. J. (2008). *Strengthening family coping resources: Multi-family group for families affected by trauma.* Unpublished manual.

Kiser, L. J., Baumgardner, B., & Dorado, J. (2010). Who are we, but for the stories we tell: Family stories and healing. *Psychological Trauma: Theory, Research, and Practice, 2*(3), 243–249.

Kiser, L. J., & Black, M. A. (2005). Family processes in the midst of urban poverty. *Aggression and Violent Behavior, 10*(6), 715–750.

Kiser, L. J., Connors, K., Gardner, S., Strieder, F., Dowling, L., & Lyons, J. (2009). *Family assessment of needs and strengths-Trauma exposure and adaptation.* Unpublished instrument and manual. Available from the authors.

Kiser, L. J., Nurse, W., Luckstead, A., & Collins, K. S. (2008). Understanding the impact of traumas on family life from the viewpoint of female caregivers living in urban poverty. *Traumatology, 14*(3), 77–90.

Kiser, L. J., Ostoja, E., & Pruitt, D. B. (1998). Dealing with stress and trauma in families. In B. Pfefferbaum (Ed.), Stress in children, *Child and Adolescent Psychiatric Clinics of North America, 7*(1), 87–104.

Kishur, G. R. (1984). *Chiasmal effects of traumatic stressors: The emotional costs of support.* Master's thesis, Purdue University, West Lafayette, IN.

Kishur, G. R., & Figley, C. R. (1987). *The relationship between psychiatric symptoms of crime victims and their supporters: Evidence of the chiasmal effects of co-victimization.* Unpublished manuscript, Purdue University, West Lafayette, IN.

Kopp, C. (1982). Antecedents of self-regulation: A developmental perspective. *Developmental Psychology, 18*, 199–214.

Laible, D. J., & Thompson, R. A. (2000). Mother–child discourse, attachment security, shared positive affect, and early conscience development. *Child Development, 71*(5), 1424–1440.

Lantz, J., & Gyamerah, J. (2002). Existential family trauma therapy. *Contemporary Family Therapy: An International Journal, 24*(2), 243–255.

Lantz, J., & Raiz, L. (2003). Play and art in existential trauma therapy with children and their parents. *Contemporary Family Therapy: An International Journal, 25*(2), 165–177.

Levis, D. J., & Hare, N. A. (1977). A review of the theoretical rationale and empirical support for the extinction approach of implosive (flooding) therapy. In M. Hersen, R. M. Eisler, & P. M. Miller (Eds.), *Progress in behavior modification: Vol. 4.* New York: Academic Press.

Levy, J. (2006). Using a metaperspective to clarify the structural-narrative debate in family therapy. *Family Process, 45*(1), 55–73.

Lindemann, E. (1944). Symptomatology and management of acute grief. *American Journal of Psychiatry, 101*, 141–148.

Litz, B. (2004). *Early intervention for trauma and traumatic loss.* New York: Guilford Press.

Loman, M., Gunnar, M.R., & the Early Experience, Stress and Neurodevelopment Center Team (2010). Early experience and the development of stress reactivity and regulation in children. *Neuroscience and Biobehavioral Reviews, 34*(6), 867–876.

Madanes, C. (1984). *Behind the one-way mirror: Advances in the practice of strategic therapy.* San Francisco: Jossey-Bass.

Mann, P. (1972). Residential mobility as an adaptive experience. *Journal of Consulting and Clinical Psychology, 39*, 37–42.

Maslach, C. (1982). *Burnout: The cost of caring.* Englewood Cliffs, NJ: Prentice Hall.

Maslach, E., & Leiter, M. P. (1997). *The truth about burnout: How organizations cause personal stress and what to do about it.* San Francisco: Jossey-Bass.

McCubbin, H., & Figley, C. R. (1983a). Bridging normative and catastrophic family stress. In H. I. McCubbin & C. R. Figley (Eds.), *Stress and the family: Vol. 1. Coping with normative transitions* (pp. xix–xxvi). New York: Brunner/Mazel.

McCubbin, H., & Figley, C. R. (1983b). Introduction. In H. I. McCubbin & C. R. Figley (Eds.), *Stress and the family: Vol. 1. Coping with normative transitions* (pp. xxi–xxxi). New York: Brunner/Mazel.

McCubbin, H. I., Joy, C., Cauble, E., Comeau, J., Patterson, J., & Needle, R. (1980). Family stress and coping: A decade review. *Journal of Marriage and the Family, 43*(4), 855–872.

McCubbin, M. A., & McCubbin, H. I. (1993). Families coping with illness: The resiliency model of family stress, adjustment, and adaptation. In C. B. Danielson, B. Hamel-Bissell, & P. Winstead-Fry (Eds.), *Families, health and illness* (pp. 21–63). St. Louis, MO: Mosby.

McCubbin, M. A., & Patterson, J. M. (1983). Family transitions: Adaptation to stress. In H. I. McCubbin & C. R. Figley (Eds.), *Stress and the family: Vol. I. Coping with normative transitions* (pp. 5–26). New York: Brunner/Mazel.

Meyers, S. A., Varkey, S., & Aguirre, A. M. (2002). Ecological correlates of family functioning. *American Journal of Family Therapy, 30*, 257–273.

Mineka, S. (1979). The role of fear in theories of avoidance learning, flooding and extinction. *Psychological Bulletin, 86*, 985–1010.

Minuchin, S. (1998). Where is the family in narrative family therapy? *Journal of Marital and Family Therapy, 24*, 397–403.

Monson, C. M., & Friedman, M. J. (2006). Back to the future of understanding trauma: Implications for cognitive-behavioral therapies for trauma. In V. M. Follette & J. I. Ruzek (Eds.), *Cognitive behavioral therapies for trauma* (pp. 1–13). New York: Guilford Press.

Montgomery, B. (1982). *Family crisis as process: Persistence and change.* Washington, DC: University Press of America.

Moreno, J. L. (1951). *Sociometry, experimental method and the science of society: An approach to a new political orientation.* Boston: Beacon House.

Morgan, A. (2000). *What is narrative therapy? An easy-to-read introduction.* Adelaide, Australia: Dulwich Centre Publications.

Mowrer, O. H. (1947). On the dual nature of learning: A reinterpretation of "conditioning" and "problem solving." *Harvard Educational Review, 17*, 102–148.

Mowrer, O. H. (1960). *Learning theory and behavior.* New York: Wiley.

Murphy, L. B., & Moriarty, A. E. (1976). *Vulnerability, coping, and growth: From infancy to adolescence.* New Haven, CT: Yale University Press.

Nader, K. O., Kriegler, J. A., Blake, D. D., & Pynoos, R. S. (1994). *Clinician Administered PTSD Scale for Children (CAPS-C).* Boston: National Centre for PTSD.

National Scientific Council on the Developing Child. (2005). *Excessive stress disrupts the architecture of the developing brain* (Working Paper No. 3). Retrieved August 9, 2012, from http://developingchild.harvard.edu/index.php/resources/reports_and_working_papers/working_papers/wp3/

NiCarthy, G., Merriam, K., & Coffman, S. (1984). *Talking it out: A guide to groups for abused women.* Seattle, WA: Seal Press.

Norris, F., Byrne, C. M., Diaz, E., & Kaniasty, K. (2001). *50,000 disaster victims speak: An empirical review of the empirical literature, 1981–2001.* Report prepared for the National Center for PTSD and the Center for Mental Health Services, White River Junction, VT.

Olson, D. H., Gorall, D. M., & Tiesel, J. W. (2007). *FACES IV manual.* Minneapolis, MN: Life Innovations.

Olson, D. H., Russell, C. S., & Sprenkle, D. H. (Eds.). (1989). *Circumplex model: Systemic assessment and treatment of families.* New York: Haworth.

Olson, D. H., Sprenkle, D. H., & Russell, C. S. (1979). Circumplex model of marital and family systems I: Cohesion and adaptability dimensions, family types, and clinical application. *Family Process, 18*, 3–28.

Osterweis, M., & Townsend, J. (1988). *Helping bereaved children: A booklet for school personnel* (DHHS Publication No. ADM 88-1553).

Parks, C. M. (1964). The effects of bereavement on physical and mental health: A study of the case records of widows. *British Medical Journal, 2*, 274.

Parks, C. M. (1972). Accuracy of predictions of survival in later stages of cancer. *British Medical Journal, 1*, 29–31.

Patterson, J. M. (1991). A family systems perspective for working with youth with disability. *Pediatrician, 18,* 129–141.

Patterson, J. M. (2002). Integrating family resilience and family stress theory. *Journal of Marriage and the Family, 64*(2), 349–360.

Peacock, E. J., & Wong, P. T. P. (1996). Anticipatory stress: The relation of locus of control, optimism, and control appraisals to coping. *Journal of Research in Personality, 30*(2), 204–222.

Perry, B. D., & Pollard, R. (1998). Homeostasis, stress, trauma, and adaptation: A neurodevelopmental view of childhood trauma. *Child and Adolescent Psychiatric Clinics of North America, 7,* 33–51.

Pilisuk, M., & Parks, S. H. (1986). *The healing web: Social networks and human survival.* Hanover, NH: University Press of New England.

Pinderhughes, E. E., Dodge, K. A., Bates, J. E., Pettit, G. S., & Zelli, A. (2000). Discipline responses: Influences of parents' socioeconomic status, ethnicity, beliefs about parenting, stress, and cognitive-emotional processes. *Journal of Family Psychology, 14*(3), 380–400.

Pinderhughes, E. E., Nix, R., Foster, E. M., & Jones, D. (2001). Parenting in context: Impact of neighborhood poverty, residential stability, public services, social networks, and danger on parental behaviors. *Journal of Marriage and the Family, 63*(4), 941–953.

Pines, A. M., Aronson, E., & Kafray, D. (1981). *Burnout: From tedium to personal growth.* New York: Free Press.

Pynoos, R., Rodriguez, N., Steinberg, A., Stuber, M., & Frederick, C. (1998). *UCLA PTSD Index for DSM-IV.*

Pynoos, R., Steinberg, A., & Aronson, L. (1997). Traumatic experiences: The early organization of memory in school-age children and adolescents. In P. Appelbaum, M. Elin, & L. Uyehara (Eds.), *Trauma and memory: Clinical and legal controversies* (pp. 272–289). New York: Oxford University Press.

Pynoos, R. S., Steinberg, A. M., & Piacentini, J. C. (1999). A developmental psychopathology model of childhood traumatic stress and intersection with anxiety disorders. *Biological Psychiatry, 46,* 1542–1554.

Rabkin, J. G., & Struening, E. L. (1976). Life events, stress, and illness. *Science, 194,* 1013–1020.

Rando, T. A. (1984). *Grief, dying, and death: Clinical interventions for caregivers.* Champaign, IL: Research Press.

Raphael, B. (1973). Bereavement: A paradigm for preventive medicine. *Sandoz Therapeutic Quarterly, 2,* 1–9.

Raphael, B. (1983). *The anatomy of bereavement.* New York: Basic Books.

Repetti, R. L., Taylor, S. E., & Seeman, T. E. (2002). Risky families: Family social environments and the mental and physical health of offspring. *Psychological Bulletin, 128*(2), 330–366.

Repetti, R. L., & Wood, J. (1997). Families accommodating to chronic stress: Unintended and unnoticed processes. In B. H. Gottlieb (Ed.), *Coping with chronic stress* (pp. 191–220). New York: Plenum Press.

Resnick, H. S., Kilpatrick, D. G., Dansky, B. S., Saunders, B. E., & Best, C. L. (1993). Prevalence of civilian trauma and posttraumatic stress disorder in a representative national sample of women. *Journal of Consulting and Clinical Psychology, 61*(6), 984–991.

Ribbe, D. (1996). *Psychometric review of Traumatic Event Screening Instrument for Children (TESI-C)*. In B. H. Stamm (Ed.), *Measurement of Stress, Trauma, and Adaptation* (pp. 386–387). Lutherville, MD: Sidran Press.

Rimm, D. C., & Masters, J. C. (1979). *Behavior therapy: Techniques and empirical findings* (2nd ed.). New York: Academic Press.

Roberts, A. R. (2005). *Traumatic stress and crisis intervention models: Crisis intervention handbook* (3rd ed.). New York: Oxford University Press.

Roth, S., Newman, E., Pelcovitz, D., Kolk, B. van der, & Mandel, F. S. (1997). Complex PTSD in victims exposed to sexual and physical abuse: Results from the DSM-IV Field Trial for Posttraumatic Stress Disorder. *Journal of Traumatic Stress, 10*(4), 539–555.

Rothschild, B. (2000). *The body remembers: The psychophysiology of trauma and trauma treatment.* London: Norton.

Russell, C. S., & Olson, D. H. (1983). Circumplex model of marital and family systems: Review of empirical support and elaboration of therapeutic process. In D. A. Bagarozzi, A. P. Jurich, & R. W. Jackson (Eds.), *Marital and family therapy: New perspectives in theory, research and practice* (pp. 25–47). New York: Human Sciences Press.

Rynearson, E. K. (Ed.). (2006). *Violent death: Resilience and intervention beyond the crisis.* New York: Routledge.

Salmon, K., & Bryant, R. A. (2002). Posttraumatic stress disorder in children: The influence of developmental factors. *Clinical Psychology Review, 22*(2), 163–188.

Scheeringa, M. S., & Zeanah, C. H. (2001). A relational perspective on PTSD in early childhood. *Journal of Traumatic Stress, 14*(4), 799–815.

Schwarz, E. D., McNally, R. J., & Yeh, L. C. (1998). The trauma response of children and adolescents: Future directions in research. *Child and Adolescent Psychiatric Clinics of North America, 7,* 229–238.

Selye, H. (1956). *Stress in life.* New York: McGraw-Hill.

Selye, H. (1974). *Stress without distress.* New York: Lippincott.

Sharpley, C., & Cross, D. (1982). A psychometric evaluation of the Spanier Dyadic Adjustment Scale. *Journal of Marriage and the Family, 44,* 730–741.

Shochet, I., & Dadds, M. (1997). When individual child psychotherapy exacerbates family systems problems in child abuse cases: A clinical analysis. *Clinical Child Psychology and Psychiatry, 2,* 239–249.

Shumaker, S. A., & Brownell, A. (1985). Introduction: Social support intervention. *Journal of Social Issues, 1,* 1–4.

Silverman, W. K., Ortiz, C. D., Viswesvaran, C., Burns, B. J., Kolko, D. J., Putnam, F. W., et al. (2008). Evidence-based psychosocial treatments for children and adolescents exposed to traumatic events. *Journal of Clinical Child and Adolescent Psychology, 37*(1), 156.

Solomon, R. L., Kamin, L. F., & Wynne, L. C. (1953). Traumatic avoidance learning: The outcomes of several extinction procedures with dogs. *Journal of Abnormal and Social Psychology, 48,* 219–302.

Solomon, R. L., & Wynne, L. C. (1954). Traumatic avoidance learning: The principles of anxiety conservation and partial irreversibility. *Psychological Review, 61,* 353–385.

Solomon, S. D., & Davidson, J. R. (1997). Trauma: Prevalence, impairment, service use and cost. *Journal of Clinical Psychiatry, 58*(Suppl. 9), 5–11.

Solomon, Z., Mikulincer, M., Fried, B., & Wosner, Y. (1987). Family characteristics of PTSD: A follow-up of Israeli combat stress reactions casualties. *Family Process, 26*(3), 383–394.

Southwick, S. M., Morgan, C. A., Vythilingam, M., Krystal, J. H., & Charney, D. S. (2004). Emerging neurobiological factors in stress resilience. *PTSD Research Quarterly, 14,* 1–3.

Spanier, G. B. (1976). Measuring dyadic adjustment: New scales for assessing the quality of marriage and similar dyads. *Journal of Marriage and the Family, 38,* 15–28.

Stamm, B. H. (1995). *Secondary traumatic stress: Self-care issues for clinicians, researchers, and educators.* Lutherville, MD: Sidran Press.

Stamm, B. H. (2006). The Professional Quality of Life Scales: A measurement for caregivers to assess the positive and negative aspects of work in the field. *The Dialogue: A Quarterly Technical Assistance Bulletin on Disaster Mental Health,* Winter, 16–19. Rockville, MD: U.S. Department of Health and Human Services, Substance Abuse and Mental Health Services Administration. Retrieved March 3, 2006, from http://www.mentalhealth.samhsa.gov/media/ken/pdf/dtac/dialoguewinter2006.pdf.

Straus, M. A., Hamby, S. L., Boney-McCoy, S., & Sugarman, D. B. (1996). The Revised Conflict Tactics Scales (CTS2): Development and preliminary psychometric data. *Journal of Family Issues, 17,* 283–316.

Sween, E. (1998). The one-minute question: What is narrative therapy? Some working answers. *Gecko, 2,* 3–6.

Tedeschi, R. G., & Calhoun, L. G. (2004). Posttraumatic growth: Conceptual foundations and empirical evidence. *Psychological Inquiry, 15*(1), 1–18.

Toth, S. L., Maughan, A., Manly, J. T., Spagnola, M., & Cicchetti, D. (2002). The relative efficacy of two interventions in altering maltreated preschool children's representational models: Implications for attachment theory. *Development and Psychopathology, 14,* 777–808.

Trimble, M. R. (1981). *Post-traumatic neurosis: From railway spine to the whiplash.* New York: Wiley.

Ursano, R. J., Bell, C., Eth, S., Friedman, M., Norwood, A., Pfefferbaum, B., et al. (2004). *Practice guideline for the treatment of patients with acute stress disorder and posttraumatic stress disorder.* Arlington, VA: American Psychiatric Association.

U.S. Department of Health and Human Services, Administration for Children and Families, Administration on Children, Youth and Families, & Children's Bureau. (2010). *Child maltreatment 2009.* Retrieved August 10, 2012, from http://www.acf.hhs.gov/programs/cb/stats_research/index.htm#can

VA/DoD Clinical Practice Guideline Working Group. (2003). *Management of post-traumatic stress.* Washington, DC: VA Office of Quality and Performance.

Veith, I. (1965). *Hysteria: The history of a disease.* Chicago: University of Chicago Press.

Walsh, F. (2003). Family resilience: A framework for clinical practice references. *Family Process, 42*(1), 1–18.

Walsh, F. (2007). Traumatic loss and major disasters: Strengthening family and community resilience. *Family Process, 46,* 207–227.

Watzlawick, P., Beavin, J. H., & Jackson, D. D. (1967). *Pragmatics of human communication: A study of interactional patterns, pathologies, and paradoxes.* New York: Norton.

Watzlawick, P., Weakland, J. H., & Fisch, R. (1974). *Change: Principles of problem formation and problem resolution.* New York: Norton.

Weathers, F. W., Litz, B. T., Herman, D. S., Huska, J. A., & Keane, T. M. (1993). *The PTSD Checklist: Reliability, validity and diagnostic utility.* Paper presented at the Annual Meeting of the International Society for Traumatic Stress Studies, San Antonio, TX.

Wethington, H. R., Hahn, R. A., Fuqua-Whitley, D. S., Sipe, T. A., Crosby, A. E., Johnson, R. L., et al. (2008). The effectiveness of interventions to reduce psychological harm from traumatic events among children and adolescents: A systematic review. *American Journal of Preventive Medicine, 35*(3), 287–313.

White, M. (1992). Deconstruction and therapy. In D. Epston & M. White (Eds.), Experience, contradiction, narrative, and imagination: Selected papers of David Epston and Michael White, 1989–1991 (pp. 109–151). Adelaide, Australia: Dulwich Centre Publications.

White, M. (2005). Children, trauma and subordinate storyline development. *International Journal of Narrative Therapy and Community Work, 3 & 4,* 10–21.

White, M., & Epston, D. (1990). *Narrative means to therapeutic ends.* New York: Norton.

Whittaker, J. K., & Garbarino, J. (1983). *Social support networks: Informal helping in the human services.* New York: Transaction.

Wilson, J. P., & Keane, T. M. (Eds.). (2004). *Assessing psychological trauma and PTSD* (2nd ed.). New York: Guilford Press.

Winje, D. (1998). Cognitive coping: The psychological significance of knowing what happened in the traumatic event. *Journal of Traumatic Stress, 11*(4), 627–643.

# Index